The diverse people who shaped an Ancient Kingdom

Men and Women of Goguryeo

The diverse people who shaped an Ancient Kingdom

Men and Women of Goguryeo

Hyun-sook Kim

NORTHEAST ASIAN
HISTORY FOUNDATION

Publisher's Note

The countries of the East Asian region have historically shared close ties. Since ancient times, various ethnic groups have emerged on East Asia and formed states. Conversely, conquest war have sometimes caused ethnic groups and states to disappear in history. Countries such as Korea, China, and Japan have evolved from ancient times to the present day, developing through conflict and war on the one hand, and through exchange and cooperation on the other. As East Asian region became civilized developed on the continent from the earliest times, they formed unique cultures through the exchange of materials and ideas. Modernity has been marked by conflicts between continental and maritime powers in East Asia, as well as invasive imperialist wars. A particularly unfortunate period in history unfolded when Japan forcibly annexed Korea and invaded China.

Peace in East Asia requires overcoming the unfortunate history of the past and establishing a new paradigm of international relations, however, unproductive nationalistic historical perspectives have tended to predominate in the early 21st century. When countries strongly emphasize a nationalistic viewpoint, distrust increases among neighboring nations, resulting in the regrettable unfortunate situation of escalating conflicts and tensions.

The Northeast Asian History Foundation was established in 2006 with the aim to resolve conflicts arising from differences in historical perceptions in the East Asian region in order to promote cooperation and prosperity within a framework of peace. Over the years, the Foundation has conducted research on East Asian history and engaged in international academic exchanges to bridge differences in historical perceptions. The results have been published in various series of historical publications and have received acclaim from many readers. However, most of these publications are in Korean, which has limited their ability to reach a global audience and facilitate cross-border communication with world citizens. Therefore, in order to share Northeast Asian History Foundation research results with the international community and create a platform for communication aiming to resolve differences in historical perceptions, the Foundation publishes the <History & Culture> Series.

The series covers topics that can help people around the world understand issues that have caused disputes in East Asian history, encompassing territorial and maritime issues, among others. We hope that this series, published by the Northeast Asian History Foundation, can make a significant contribution to the understanding of historical conflicts and the bridge of differences in historical perceptions in the East Asian region.

Young-ho Lee

President of Northeast Asian History Foundation

Preface

While studying ancient Korean history, especially the kingdom of Goguryeo history, I have tried to understand the organizations, ruling systems and operating principles of ancient states. I have struggled with a limited number of lines scribbled in ancient sources, trying to piece them together like a jigsaw puzzle to find out what happened so long ago that I can hardly even imagine it. Although my main focus has been on the systems and organizations of ancient kingdoms, I have also found myself wondering about the people who were part of them. I could not help but be curious about what the Goguryeo people thought and how they lived. This made me realize that I wanted to write about the Goguryeo people themselves, as individuals. I wanted to find out how they reacted to certain historical events and whether their minds worked differently from ours today.

Writing about people mentioned in historical sources is no easy task, however. The atmosphere has changed considerably in recent years, but there was a time when writing anything other than research papers was frowned upon. Scholars who presented many papers and wrote the occasional miscellaneous piece were praised, but academia disapproved of those who presented few papers and wrote more for the general public. Furthermore, it is truly a task that requires expertise to present the stories of historical figures, which inevitably carry the weight of history, in terms that are easy for everyone to understand. It requires an understanding of life across time and finely honed writing skills that can engage the public. Perhaps these aspects have delayed the publication of this book.

This book introduces the history and society of Goguryeo through stories about its people. It was written so that students and the general public could get an overview of the Goguryeo history through the stories of people involved in the establishment, growth, and fall of the kingdom. Explanations have been added as much as possible, but only to the extent that supporting evidence allow. Almost all available sources related to Goguryeo have been consulted, but much information has been extracted from the *History of the Three Kingdoms* (『三國史記』).

What sets this book apart from other history books is the creation of a separate section dedicated to female figures in Goguryeo. Nowadays, there is a saying "history" vs. "herstory," but traditionally, history has been a predominantly male-centric narrative. However, despite the limited records, there are many intriguing female figures in Goguryeo who may not have taken center stage, but had a significant impact on history. It is worth noting that Goguryeo women, uninfluenced by Confucian logic, were quite enterprising, positive, and assertive in their thinking and attitude toward life. Hoping to provide an opportunity to discover a new perspective on Goguryeo through these women, the book is structured as "Men and Women in Goguryeo History. It would be interesting to compare the thoughts and way of life of the Goguryeo people, both men and women, with our present selves.

November 2023

Hyun-sook Kim

Contents

Notes

1. This book is a translation of 『고구려 남자, 고구려 여자–고구려를 이룬 다양한 사람들』 (Northeast Asian History Foundation, 2019).
2. If it is not possible to identify an existing English transliteration of a Korean name or place, it is transliterated according to the guidelines provided by the Ministry of Culture, Sports and Tourism of the Republic of Korea.

I

Goguryeo Men, Symbols of Valor and Zeal

1.
Jumong's Companions: Oi, Mari, and Hyeopbo

One must overcome many difficulties to become a hero revered by all, and almost no one manages to do so completely on their own. Most heroes need support from their friends, siblings, or vassals. Such was the case with the heroes of the ancient Korean kingdom Goguryeo (37 BCE–668 CE). When Jumong escaped Buyeo and established Goguryeo near the Biryu River, Oi (烏伊), Mari (摩離), and Hyeopbo (陜父) were by his side.

This is how their story is described in *Annals of Goguryeo*,[1] a part of the *History of the Three Kingdoms*:

With his friends Oi, Mari, and Hyeopbo, Jumong reached

1 『高句麗本紀』

> the Eomsa River, or Gaesa River, northeast of today's Aprok River. However, they could not cross the river because there was no bridge. Fearing that the pursuing Buyeo troops would catch up with them, Jumong called out to the water, "I am the son of the Emperor of Heaven[2] and the maternal grandson of Habaek,[3] the River God. I ran away from Buyeo today, and my pursuers are on their way. What shall I do?" And the fish and turtles rose to the surface and formed a bridge for him to cross the river.

Although Oi's name is spelled "Joi (烏伊)" in a 1512 copy of the *History of the Three Kingdoms*, this seems to have been an error caused by the addition of an extra stroke to the character "烏" when the woodblock was carved, since the name is spelled "Oi" in other parts of the *History of the Three Kingdoms*, such as the descriptions of the first and sixth years of the reign of Dongmyeong the Holy King.[4] The name Oi also appears in other sources, such as the section on Goguryeo in Volume 1 of the *Memoirs of the Three Kingdoms*[5] and the section on 37 BCE in Volume 1 of the *Essentials from the*

2 天帝

3 河伯, It is the deity of water that appears in the founding myth of Goguryeo. In the Moduru Tomb stele, it is written as "Habak (河泊)."

4 東明聖王

5 『三國遺事』

History of the Three Kingdoms.[6] Unlike *History of the Three Kingdoms*, which names all three of his friends who accompanied Jumong to the middle basin of the Aprok River, *Memoirs of the Three Kingdoms* does not mention Mari or Hyeopbo. The names of the friends also vary in different historical sources. The story of Goguryeo in Volume 100 of the *Book of Wei*[7] states that the two friends who traveled south with Jumong were Oin (烏引) and Owi (烏違). Meanwhile, the story of Goguryeo recorded in Volume 94 of the *History of the Northern Dynasties*[8] says that Jumong was accompanied by Eonwi (馬黎) and two others. According to the *Annals of Baekje*[9] in Book 13 of the *History of the Three Kingdoms*, when King Onjo,[10] the founder of Baekje (18 BCE–660 CE), fled south from Goguryeo, he was accompanied by ten subjects, including Ogan (烏干) and Mari (馬黎). It is interesting to note that the pronunciation of Ogan is similar to that of Oi. The name Mari is also pronounced exactly the same as the Mari mentioned in *Annals of Goguryeo*, although they are based on different Chinese characters. Scholars consider this phenomenon of characters with similar pronunciations being portrayed as friends of the founders who contributed to the establishment of Goguryeo and

6 『三國史節要』

7 『魏書』

8 『北史』

9 『百濟本紀』

10 溫祚王

Baekje to be analogous to the origin myths of Buyeo and Goguryeo, whose narratives share the same name "Dongmyeong (東明)" as their founders. The fact that the founder of Buyeo is called King Dongmyeong,[11] and the founder of Goguryeo (Jumong) is called Dongmyeong the Holy King, suggests that they all have their roots in the same Buyeo myth, and the narratives of Jumong's southward migration and Onjo's southward journey also reflect their derivation from the Buyeo myth.

Moreover, the major powers that supported the founding of both Goguryeo and Baekje all had ancestral ties to the Yemaek (濊貊) tribe, and since both kingdoms originated in Buyeo, it seems possible that their founding myths borrowed certain aspects from Buyeo's. However, there is another possibility worth considering: what if Oi and Mari of Goguryeo and Ogan and Mari of Baekje were not the names of specific individuals, but rather the names of specific government offices?

When King Yuri left Buyeo for Goguryeo, he also traveled with friends. He retrieved a piece of a broken blade that Jumong had hidden under a pillar, and then went to Jolbon with Okji (屋智), Guchu (句鄒), and Dojo (都祖). However, these names bear no resemblance to Oi, Mari, or Hyeopbo in either pronunciation or meaning. What Jumong and Yuri had in common was that they both suffered perse-

11 東明王

cution in Buyeo before fleeing with three friends to the central area of the Aprok River basin. Jumong and his friends founded Goguryeo, while Yuri and his friends came to the kingdom founded by his father where Yuri became its crown prince and eventually succeeded his father as the second king of Goguryeo.

Jumong's and Yuri's friends, on the other hand, seem to be very different. While the records of the exploits of Oi, Mari, and Hyeopbo extend into the reign of King Yuri, there is no record of the whereabouts of Okji, Guchu, and Dojo beyond their journey from Buyeo to Goguryeo. In the tenth month of 32 BCE, the sixth year of the reign of Dongmyeong the Holy King, Oi and Bubunno received orders from the king to attack Haenginguk (荇人國), a state southeast of Mt. Taebaek. The conquered land was then turned into a fortified city of Goguryeo. In the eighth month of the 33rd year of King Yuri's reign (14 CE), Oi and Mari led 20,000 troops to the west and conquered a tribe called Yangmaek (梁貊). They also attacked Goguryeo Prefecture (高句麗縣), which had been established by the Han Dynasty of China to keep Goguryeo in check. Oi and Mari thus achieved a number of military triumphs.

Hyeopbo, on the other hand, was in charge of internal affairs in Goguryeo. According to *Annals of Goguryeo* in the *History of the Three Kingdoms*, Hyeopbo served as the Daebo[12] in the 22nd year of

12 大輔, present-day Prime Minister

King Yuri's reign (3 CE). Although domestic conditions had not yet been adjusted to the recent relocation of the kingdom's capital, King Yuri immersed himself in hunting. When Hyeopbo advised him to pay more attention to the livelihood of his people, the king ignored Hyeopbo, who had been his father's friend and helped to found the kingdom. Instead, King Yuri stripped Hyeopbo of his title of Daebo and put him to work tending the garden. Enraged, Hyeopbo fled south to one of the Three Han confederations.[13] This story suggests that Daebo was the highest ranking official in Goguryeo, overseeing the political operations of the state.

These details support the possibility that the names Oi, Mari, and Hyeopbo who accompanied Jumong, as well as those of Okji, Guchu, and Dojo who accompanied Yuri, may have referred to government positions in charge of military and political affairs during the early stages of the Goguryeo state, rather than to specific individuals. This also implies that the ten aides, including Ogan and Mari, who accompanied Onjo when he fled Goguryeo may have been the roles they held rather than their personal names. In other words, the references to companions who contributed to the establishment of Goguryeo and Baekje may serve as evidence that the division of governmental offices existed, albeit in a rudimentary form, in the two ancient kingdoms.

13 南韓, It refers the entire or partial region of the Three Han Confederations in the central and southern parts of the Korean Peninsula.

2.
The Loyal Subjects: Milwu and Yuyu

Shin Sung-gyeom: A Goryeo Loyalist Who Swapped Clothes with King Wang Geon and Died in His Place

Shin Sung-gyeom (申崇謙, 882–927) was born in Pyeongsan, a county in today's Hwanghaebuk-do, where his family originated. However, the *History of Goryeo*[14] says that his birthplace was Gwanghaeju, in present-day Chuncheon. His childhood name was Neungsan (能山), and his posthumous name was Jangjeol (壯節). He grew up to be a brave man blessed with a strong physique. Together with Hong Yu (洪儒), Bae Hyeon-gyeong (裵玄慶, d. 936) and Bok Ji-

14 『高麗史』

gyeom (卜智謙), Shin Sung-gyeom overthrew Gung Ye (r. 901–918), the founder of the Taebong(泰封), and crowned Wang Geon (王建, r. 918–943) as king, leading to the fall of Taebong and the establishment of the Goryeo Dynasty in 918. He was thus recognized as a major contributor to the establishment of the new kingdom and was appointed Grand General.[15]

In 927, the tenth year of King Wang Geon's reign, Shin Sung-gyeom was killed in action at Dongsu (桐藪) near Mt. Gong (today's Mt. Palgong, Gyeongsangbuk-do), where he was engaged in fierce combat with the Hu Baekje[16] troops led by Gyeon Hweon (甄萱, 867–936). When the king was surrounded by the Hu Baekje troops and the situation became critical, Shin fought back with all his might to secure an escape route for the king before meeting his own death on the battlefield alongside Won Bo and Kim Rak. To express his gratitude, the king conferred the rank of Wonyun[17] on Shin's younger brother Neunggil and his son Bo, and built Jimyo Temple (智妙寺) on Mt. Palgong for the repose of his loyal subjects. Later, in 994, the 13th year of the reign of King Seongjong (r. 981–997), Shin was posthumously given the title of Meritorious Subject for Founding a New Dynasty[18] and his tomb was moved to Wang Geon Shrine. King Yejong of Go-

15 大將軍

16 後百濟

17 元尹, It held the 10th rank among the sixteen grades of local officials in Goguryeo. It was a rank rather than an actual post.

18 開國 壯節公

ryeo (r. 1105–1122) even composed a Silla Hyangga[19] titled "Chant for Two Great Generals"[20] in honor of Shin Sung-gyeom and Kim Rak.

Although there are no surviving sources that describe the details of the battle between Goryeo and Hu Baekje forces at Mt. Gong, various myths and stories about the battle have been passed down in the Daegu area. At the time, Hu Baekje was pressuring Silla, and when its forces threatened Silla's capital, Seorabeol, Goryeo troops marched south to support Silla. From Mutae, an area in present-day Seobyeon-dong, Buk-gu, City of Daegu, the Goryeo troops moved northeast along Donghwa Stream and passed through Yeongyeong.[21] They continued east through Jimyo-dong and Midae-dong until they clashed with the Hu Baekje troops, who were staying at Donghwa Temple, somewhere near Baegan-dong or Naehak-dong. According to Gyeon Hweon's biography in the *History of the Three Kingdoms*, "the troops at Dongsu (Donghwa Temple) fled in all directions at the sight of the Goryeo army banner when Wang Geon arrived at Mt. Gong," suggesting that Goryeo had the upper hand in the early stages of the war.

In Seobyeon-dong, Daegu, there is a place called Mutae,[22] which means "no laziness" in Korean. It is said to have been named after

19 鄕歌, The collective term for songs created in their local letters during the Silla (新羅) Dynasty period.

20 「悼二將歌」

21 硏經

22 無怠

King Wang Geon, who told his soldiers to be vigilant and not lax in their duties, and another theory is that when Wang Geon passed by this place, he saw that the locals were diligent and not lax, so he named it Mutae. Following Donghwa Stream northeast from there leads to a town called Yeongyeong. Yeongyeong, which means "studying literature" in Korean, is said to have been named by Wang Geon because he could hear the sound of scholars reading when he passed through it.

After passing safely below Donghwa Temple at Mt. Palgong, the Goryeo troops crossed Neungseong Hill and advanced toward Yeongcheon to defeat the Hu Baekje troops. According to the *Newly Expanded Geographical Survey of the Eastern Kingdom*,[23] the battle between the Goryeo and Hu Baekje forces took place at Taejoji in Yeongcheon. Located about 12 kilometers from Yeongcheon-gun, Taejoji is believed to be near the entrance to Eunhae Temple. The Goryeo troops lost the battle and were forced to retreat along the same route they had taken in pursuit of the enemy.

After their defeat at Taejoji, the Goryeo troops retreated along the Donghwa Stream toward Jimyo-dong and regrouped at present-day Sallae (箭灘), where the Seobyeon Stream joins the Geumho River. There is a hill between Jimyo 1-dong and Jimyo 3-dong called the Trumpet Hill, which was named after the trumpet sounded by the

---

23 『新增東國輿地勝覽』

Hu Baekje troops as they crossed the hill to announce their defeat of Goryeo. The name Sallae also comes from a battle scene in which the stream of arrows fired by the Goryeo and Hu Baekje troops across the creek formed a river.

As the two sides faced each other at Sallae, reinforcements led by Shin Sung-gyeom and Kim Rak arrived. The Goryeo forces pushed the Hu Baekje forces back to the entrance of Miri Temple. The site is located at the foot of Mt. Wang in Jimyo-dong, between the roads leading up from Pagunjae to Donghwa and Pagye Temples, respectively. Today, a statue of Shin Sung-gyeom stands there next to a stele inscribed with *Site of Goryeo's Loyal General Shin's Death*,[24] commemorating the loyal death of the Goryeo General.

King Dongcheon's Subjects Milwu and Yuyu

On the verge of being annihilated by the Hu Baekje forces surrounding them, Shin Sung-gyeom swapped clothes with King Wang Geon. This tricked the enemy into thinking that Shin was the king, ultimately costing him his life while the real king managed to escape. The story of how Shin became a symbol of loyalty in Goryeo is reminiscent of another story from centuries earlier, when Milwu and Yuyu

24 『高麗壯節申公殉節之地』

offered their lives to save King Dongcheon (r. 227–248) of Goguryeo.

After invading Goguryeo in 244 and capturing Hwando Fortress the following year, the Wei General Guan Qiujian (毌丘儉, d. 255), who also served as governor of Youzhou,[25] ordered the Xuantu Commander[26] Wang Qi (王頎) to pursue King Dongcheon. The Goguryeo king hastily fled to southern Okjeo, but most of the troops accompanying him had dispersed by the time they reached the Juk Peak (most likely present-day Hwangcho Peak). Milwu, who was born in Dongbu (東部), was willing to risk his own life and told the king to flee while he halted the enemy's advance. Milwu then organized a group of soldiers and attacked the enemy's camp, but fell in battle. After narrowly escaping through a side road, the king rallied his remaining troops and declared, "Whoever brings Milwu back will be generously rewarded." A soldier named Yu Okgu from Habu stepped forward and volunteered to make the attempt. Yu rushed to the battlefield and returned with Milwu slumped over his back. The king laid him on his lap, and after some time, Milwu finally regained consciousness.

The pursuit by Wei's troops never ceased. King Dongcheon was too desperate to come up with a plan, and a man from Dongbu named Yuyu stepped forward and said, "We may be in great danger, but we can't die in vain. I will go and offer food to the Wei troops and look for an opportunity to stab their commander to death." Yuyu

25 幽州刺史

26 玄菟太守

took the food to the enemy camp and pretended to surrender. When he approached the commander, he pulled out a knife hidden under a plate of food and stabbed him to death before taking his own life. The death of their commander threw the Wei troops into disarray, and King Dongcheon took the opportunity to attack the Wei troops from three directions, throwing them into confusion until they retreated to Nakrang (樂浪).

Thanks to his loyal men, King Dongcheon was able to survive the crisis and regain control of his kingdom. After the war, the king generously rewarded his subjects according to their contributions. He gave Geogok and Cheongmokgok as fiefdoms to Milwu, who had contributed the most. As for Yuyu, the king posthumously promoted him to the rank of Gusaja (九使者) and gave his son Dawu the rank of Daesaja (大使者).[27] To Yu Okgu, who had risked his life to save Milwu, the king gave the land called Amnokwon and Dunulhawon[28] as fiefdoms. This story of subjects who did not hesitate to risk their lives for their king, and of a king who let a subject rest his head on his lap until he regained consciousness, vividly shows mutual trust and loyalty. The strong bonds they shared were revealed once again when King Dongcheon passed away.

After the death of King Dongcheon, everyone in the kingdom

27 Gusaja and Daesaja are ranks that only appeared during the 20th year reign of King Dongcheon in the early period of Goguryeo.

28 鴨淥原·杜訥河原

was saddened by the memory of the deceased king's virtue, and many of those who had served him closely were willing to follow him to the grave. His successor, King Jungcheon (r. 248–270), discouraged them from doing so, saying that it would be disrespectful. Nevertheless, some sneaked up to the king's tomb on the day of his funeral and killed themselves. Their bodies were covered with brushwood, and the place was named Brushwood Hill.[29] Sadly, stories of such a caring king and subjects loyal enough to risk their lives for him are now considered legends to be found only in history books.

29 柴原

3.
For the Glory of Goguryeo and the Family: Yeommo and Moduru

Whose Tomb Is It? Yeommo or Moduru?

Goguryeo's second capital was in present-day Ji'an (集安) in China's Jilin-sheng, which faces the North Korean city of Manpo from across the Aprok River. The proximity of the two cities makes it possilbe to see the trucks that occasinally pass through Manpo from Ji'an and people fishing in the river. The number of tourists visiting Ji'an has increased since the ancient Goguryeo ruins, such as Gungnae (Guonei) City,[30] the Tomb Stele of King Gwanggaeto,[31] and the royal tombs, including the Tomb of the General,[32] and the Taewang-

30 國內城
31 廣開土大王陵碑
32 將軍塚

neug,[33] were listed as UNESCO World Heritage Sites. After visiting these historical sites, tourists can take a cruise that approaches the other side of the river and sometimes they wave or cheer at the North Koreans. Some of the North Koreans wave back cheerfully, but at other times they show unhappy expressions.

A 20-minute drive toward the Unbong Dam reveals some fish farms along the Aprok River on the right, and a little further down are the Hahaebang Ancient Tombs. A survey conducted in 1962 found nearly 50 Goguryeo tombs, but only about 30 remain today.

Corn and grapes now grow where the tombs once stood. Within this cornfield is a mid-fifth century Goguryeo earthen mound tomb with a stone chamber, 22 meters in diameter, 70 meters in circumference, and four meters high. The mound is surrounded by a barbed-wire fence to prevent trespassing, and there is a marker stone in front of it stating that the tomb belongs to Yeommo (冉牟). In September 1935, a Chinese middle school teacher in Ji'an named Wang Yonglin reported to the Manchukuo government that there were letters engraved in the tomb. The next day, Jin Yufu (金毓黻), a Chinese scholar working for the Manchukuo Ministry of Education, came to examine the inscriptions, followed by Japanese scholar Ikeuchi Hiroshi (池内宏). At that time, they called the site Moduru's Tomb, but after Chinese scholar Lao Gan (勞幹) published a research paper in 1940

33 太王陵

arguing that it belonged to Yeommo, the Chinese began to call it Yeommo's Tomb. Korean and Japanese scholars, on the other hand, still refer to it as Moduru's. What caused this discrepancy?

Who Lies in the Tomb, Yeommo or Moduru?

Differences in opinions about the identity of the owner of the tomb reflect who is seen as the figures mentioned in the epitaph written in ink on the upper wall of the burial chamber. This epitaph consists of 800 characters: 80 per horizontal line and ten per vertical line. When the epitaph was first discovered, many of the characters were faint and damaged, leaving only about 400 legible. When the tomb was flooded after a heavy rain in 1994, Professor Geng Tiehua (耿鐵華) of Tonghua Normal University[34] entered the tomb and participated in the repair, increasing the number of legible characters to 436.

The first line of the epitaph contains the phrase *Daesaja Moduru* (大使者牟頭婁). This phrase is taken as the title of the epitaph by scholars who believe that the owner of the tomb was Moduru. On the other hand, scholars who believe that Yeommo was the owner of the tomb identify the first character in the second line as "mun" (文), which gives them reason to argue that Moduru was named in the

34 通化師範學院

first line because he was the author of the epitaph. Yeommo's name appears several times in the first half of the epitaph, so scholars have argued that the tomb belongs to him and that Moduru was either the author of the epitaph or a man who served Yeommo. Another reason why scholars still debate whether the tomb belonged to Yeommo or Moduru is that the epitaph seems to contain too much detail about Yeommo to believe that Moduru is the one buried there.

Layout and Content of the Epitaph

Among scholars who have studied the epitaph to date, the interpretation by Korean Scholar Noh Tae-don, published in Volume 1 of *Ancient Korean Epigraphs* (韓國古代金石文, 1992), is the best known. Let's examine the layout of the epitaph based on Noh's version:

1. 大使者牟頭婁(下缺)
2. □(下缺)
3. 河泊之孫日月之子鄒牟
4. 聖王元出北夫餘天下四
5. 方知此國郡最聖亻 □□
6. 治此郡之嗣治□□□聖
7. 王奴客祖先□□□北夫
8. 餘隨聖王來奴客△□△

9. 之故□□□□□□□

10. 世遭官恩□□□△□上

11. 聖太王之世△□□□△

12. 祀□△□□□□□□□

13. 非宀枝□□□□□□□

14. 叛逆糸 □之△□□□△

15. 冉牟□△□□△△□□

16. 遣招□□□□□□□□

17. 拘雞□□□□□□□□

18. 曁農□□□□□□□□

19. 忄 □□□□□□□□□

20. 恩亻 □△□□□□□□

21. 官客之□□□□□□冉

22. 牟令彡靈□□□□□□

23. 慕容鮮卑□氵 使人□知

24. 河泊之孫日月之子所生

25. 之地來□北夫餘大兄冉

26. 牟扌 □□公△彡□□□

27. △△□□□□□□□□

28. 牟婁□□□□□□□

29. 命遣□□□△□□□□

30. □□□□□□守□□□

31. □□□□□△□□□□

32. □□□□□造世□□□

33. □□□□□苑□□□□

34. □□□□□△□□□□

35. □□△△△△□□□□

36. □△河□□□□□□□

37. □夫△□□□□□□□

38. □河泊日月之△□□□

39. □□△祖大兄冉牟壽盡

40. □□於彼喪亡糹 由祖父

41. □□大兄慈△大兄□□

42. □世遭官恩恩祖之△

43. 道城民谷民幷領前王□

44. 育如此遝至國□上大開

45. 土地好太聖王緣祖父亻

46. 尒恩敎奴客牟頭婁□□

47. 牟敎遣令北夫餘守事河

48. 泊之孫日月之子聖王□

49. □□△昊天不弔奄便△

50. △□奴客在遠哀切如若

51. 日不□□月不□明△△

52. △□□□□□□□□□

53. □□□□□國□□□□

54. 知□△△在遠之□□□

55. 遝□□敎之□△□□□

56. □潤太隊踊躍□□□□

57. △令教老奴客□□□□

58. 官恩緣□□道□□□□

59. 使△西□□□□□□□

60. □極言教△心□□□□

61. □□□△□□□□□述

62. □□□□□□□□□□

63. □□□△不□□□□□

64. □△△△□□□□□□

65. □□□一□□□□□□

66. □△依如若□△□□□

67. 知△△□□△□□□□

68. 可△△□如△□□□□

69. □□□朔月□□□□□

70. □□□△△□□□□□

Noh's version was based on photographs of the epitaph included in the book titled *T'ung-kou* (通溝), with the lines after line 70 omitted because they were completely illegible. The lines have been rearranged into a horizontal formation in the image above, although they were originally written vertically. The triangles represent characters that Noh could not identify, although they had previously been identified by others, while the squares represent characters that are legible but cannot be identified.

Lines 1 and 2 convey the title of the epitaph. Lines 3 to 11 describe how Moduru's ancestor, who was from northern Buyeo, traveled south with Jumong, and how he and his family were allowed to work for the kings for generations until the reign of King △Gangsangseong (△□上聖太王之世).[35] Lines 12 to 40 describe the contributions Yeommo made during a rebellion and during an attack by the Murong Xianbei tribe,[36] for which he was rewarded with control of northern Buyeo. According to the last two characters in line 40 (祖父) and the phrase 大兄慈△大兄 in line 41, Yeommo's descendants continued to benefit from his contributions for generations after his death by being appointed to administrative positions in the districts, where they ruled over the people.[37]

Moduru is discussed starting in line 44. He became a local government official in northern Buyeo during the reign of King Gwanggaeto (r. 391–413).[38] The specific mention of his position, the Administrator of Northern Buyeo (令北夫餘守事),[39] differs from the description of Yeommo, which only mentions his rank.

Yeommo seems to have been given the fiefdom of northern Buyeo rather than being a local official, because he was a native of northern Buyeo and had distinguished himself in suppressing a rebel-

35 △□上聖太王之世

36 慕容鮮卑

37 城民谷民

38 國□上大開土地好太聖王

39 令北夫餘守事

lion and in the war with the Murong Xianbei. Moduru, on the other hand, was an official sent to northern Buyeo by the central government during the reign of King Gwanggaeto and served until the reign of King Jangsu (r. 413–491). When King Gwanggaeto died, Moduro mourned from afar. He must have been old by then, since he refers to himself as "an old servant." Some argue that the owner of the tomb is Moduru because Yeommo would not have called himself an old servant, but Moduru would have called himself that because he was a subject of Yeommo. However, Moduru would have called himself an old servant because he was a subject of King Gwanggaeto.

Considering that thirty-eight lines of the epitaph are dedicated to Yeommo and thirty-six lines to Moduru, the Chinese scholars' conclusion that Yeommo is the owner of the tomb does not seem far-fetched. However, assuming that the first line is the title of the epitaph and looking at the rest, it seems more reasonable to conclude that the rest of the text is dedicated to Moduru. It can be seen that the progenitor of Moduru's family accompanied Jumong in his migration south from northern Buyeo, while Yeommo, a more recent ancestor of Moduru, revived the family by making great contributions to the defense of the country. Then, Moduru himself was fortunate enough to serve King Gwanggaeto and be appointed as the official governor of northern Buyeo, the land of his ancestors, as it is said. In this context, it is reasonable to see the tomb and epitaph as belonging to Moduru, with Yeommo appearing in the epitaph as an ancestor in the middle who strengthened the reputation of Moduru's family.

When did Yeommo's Activities Take Place?

According to the epitaph, Yeommo was highly respected for suppressing a rebellion and became the middle progenitor who restored the reputation of the Moduru family by defeating the Murong Xianbei when they invaded northern Buyeo. However, scholars disagree on when these achievements of Yeommo took place. Most scholars believe that Yeommo defeated the Murong Xianbei around 346. Seeking to expand eastward, Murong Huang (297–348)[40] set out to invade Goguryeo in 339 and destroyed the mountain fortress of Hwando Fortress[41] in 342. In 345, Murong Ke[42] attacked Namso Fortress[43] before invading Buyeo the following year. These incidents of aggression made the defense of its border with northern Buyeo a pressing matter for Goguryeo, and Yeommo seems to have been chosen to handle it.

In my opinion, however, Yeommo defeated the Murong Xianbei in 285. This estimate is based on a research paper I wrote in 1997 on

40 慕容皝
41 丸都城
42 慕容恪
43 南蘇城

the mid-to-late Goguryeo system of local government. After reconsidering the estimate more than 20 years later, my conclusion remains unchanged for two reasons. One is the episode of treason that Yeommo suppressed. While historical sources do not mention a rebellion during the reign of King Gogukwon (r. 331–371),[44] there is mention of princes rebelling under King Seocheon (r. 270–292),[45] who ruled almost a century earlier. The other reason is that when Murong Huang invaded Goguryeo in 342, he carried off the body of King Micheon (r. 300–331)[46] and kidnapped King Gogukwon's mother. In order to get his mother back, King Gogukwon had no choice but to humble himself before the Former Yan Dynasty (337–370)[47] by sending envoys to the Yan and receiving a peerage from them. In other words, Goguryeo was unable to counterattack when the Murong Xianbei attacked Buyeo in 346, and remained incapable of actively responding to national threats for some time. It seems more reasonable to conclude that Yeommo made a major contribution when Goguryeo and the Murong force attempted to invade Buyeo, taking advantage of the chaotic time in the kingdom.

At that time, northern Buyeo had not been incorporated into Goguryeo yet, because Euira (依羅), the new king of Buyeo, received

---

44 故國原王

45 西川王

46 美川王

47 燕

support from the Southern Chinese Jin Dynasty's Colonel of the East Tribe[48] to defeat Murong Hui's forces and recapture the capital of Buyeo. Even after regaining its territory, Buyeo continued to be attacked by Murong Xianbei while also facing pressure from Goguryeo, so it eventually moved its capital to Nungan.[49] These circumstances suggest that Goguryeo had already begun to occupy some areas of Buyeo by the end of the third century, although Buyeo was not completely incorporated into Goguryeo territory until after the fourth century.

Northern Buyeo, centered around modern-day Jilin, was brought to the brink of collapse by Murong Hui's attack in 285, the sixth year of Jin Dynasty's Jin Taikang era.[50] The surviving forces went to Northern Okjeo to establish Eastern Buyeo. Therefore, when Murong Xianbei attacked Buyeo, it was impossible to establish Eastern Buyeo without the support of Goguryeo. Goguryeo invaded part of the area when Buyeo was attacked by Murong Xianbei, and at the same time led some of the Buyeo troops to what was once northern Okjeo, an area under Goguryeo rule, and allowed them to settle there. According to the Tomb Stele of King Gwanggaeto, Goguryeo regarded Eastern Buyeo as a vassal state like Baekje and Silla. Thus, it seems that Goguryeo clashed with the Murong Xianbei several times over

48 東夷校尉府

49 農安

50 晉太康

the possession of Buyeo, and that Yeommo made a significant contribution during these clashes.

The Goguryeo Founding Myth in Moduru's Tomb

The body of the epitaph in Moduru's tomb begins by explaining that his ancestor accompanied the founding king of Goguryeo from northern Buyeo: "The Sage King Chumo,[51] grandson of the River God Habak[52] and son of the sun and moon, was born in northern Buyeo so that the sanctity of the village and the state would be known throughout the world..."

In the fifth century, Goguryeo made its founding myth known at home and abroad. The myth emphasized that Goguryeo was ruled by the descendants of its sacred ancestor Jumong, the son of Heaven God and maternal grandson of the River God, who had traveled south from Northern Buyeo to establish the kingdom. This was written at the beginning of the inscription on the Tomb Stele of King Gwanggaeto and was also recorded in the classic Chinese historical text, the *Book of Wei*. The Goguryeo kings were referred to with glorified titles such as "Great King (太王) ," "Holy Great King (聖太王)," or "Very Great Holy King (好太聖王)," which emphasized that the kings

51 鄒牟 聖王

52 河泊 or 河伯

had great power and that their kingdom was prosperous and powerful. Such titles emphasized the idea that the king and the royal family were born holy and thus different from everyone else, including the general nobles of Goguryeo.

The epitaph of Moduru, a government official who served in northern Buyeo during the reign of King Gwanggaeto, was probably meant to emphasize the fact that he was a descendant of a highly respected family with close ties to the royal family by mentioning that his ancestors and the founder of the kingdom came from northern Buyeo together. It was also meant to honor Moduru, who served as Administrator of Northern Buyeo (令北夫餘守事) by praising Northern Buyeo as a sacred place where the Sage King Chumo and Moduru's ancestor had been born, as well as related to Yeommo, an ancestor who had been of great service to the kingdom.

Moduru had lived in a world where pride and affection for the king could be a source of pride for oneself and one's family. Therefore, even a minor aristocrat like Moduru sought to establish a connection between his family and the founder of Goguryeo and to make it known through the epitaph on his grave.

If we could momentarily shift the topic of discussion, since the mid-1990s, a number of Goguryeo fortifications have been excavated in the area of Mt. Acha above the Han River of the Korean Peninsula. Among the excavated relics is a flat plate with the characters Yeommo (冉牟) engraved on it with a pointed object such as a nail.

The majority opinion is that this plate was made in the middle of the sixth century. Assuming that Goguryeo occupied the area during the reign of King Gwanggaeto, it seems that the Goguryeo troops must have begun building fortifications there around that time. However, more elaborate fortifications must have been built later, in the sixth century, when the forces of Baekje and Silla began to fight back. Therefore, the Goguryeo fortifications discovered today along the Han River were probably completed by the middle of the sixth century. In any case, the plate seems to have been made and used much later than Yeommo's time. But if so, why was his name engraved on it? Was it common for later generations to decorate objects with the names of famous heroes? Or did the object belong to a descendant of Moduru? This intriguing plate bearing Yeommo's name is now in the Seoul National University Museum.

4.
A Political Refugee's Portrait: Jin

A Portrait with a Vacant Space Beside It

In 2004, North Korea and China jointly registered the Goguryeo archaeological sites as a UNESCO World Heritage site. The sites in China included royal burial mounds, such as the Tomb of King Gwanggaeto and the General's Tomb, the Tomb Stele of King Gwanggaeto, the Gungnae Fortress, and the Hwando Mountain Fortress in Ji'an as well as the Onyeo Mountain Fortress in Huanren. In North Korea, a complex of Goguryeo tombs was listed, some of which contain murals in their burial chambers.

The murals on the walls of an early tomb in North Korea usually depict a portrait of the tomb's owner along with scenes from his daily life, such as depictions of him at work, outings, performances, or with guests at home. Paintings on tomb ceilings, on the other hand, often depict the gods of the sun and moon, constellations, sacred imaginary creatures, and Taoist hermits. Over time, the Goguryeo tomb walls began to depict, in fluid strokes and vivid colors, the four guardian deities—the blue dragon, white tiger, red phoenix, and black turtle—instead of scenes from everyday life. Approximately 120 Goguryeo tomb murals have survived to this day, and the fascinating sights they contain can be experienced through various catalogs and photo collections.

Perhaps the most intriguing of these murals is one of the two portraits inside a Goguryeo tomb at Deokheung-ri. The portrait on the north wall of the burial chamber shows the owner of the tomb, but there is a large blank space to the right. This void is noticeable because all the other walls, ceilings, and corridors in the tomb are covered with wall paintings. Considering the portraits in other tombs, the empty space in this tomb should be occupied by a painting of the tomb owner's wife. Meanwhile, in another mural depicting a procession in which the man is traveling, his upper body can be seen in a chariot, but the chariot behind him, in which his wife should be sitting, is empty. How is it that there is no trace of her in any of the tomb murals?

The Portrait of the Tomb Owner Couple at Deokheung-ri

The void next to the portrait of the tomb's owner should have been filled by a portrait of his wife.

The Portrait of the Tomb Owner at Deokheung-ri

Portrayals of Goguryeo Custom

Inside, beyond the entrance, the Goguryeo tomb at Deokheung-ri consists of two chambers: the antechamber and the main burial chamber. Each chamber has a vaulted ceiling that gradually narrows to a stepped ceiling consisting of two tiers in the antechamber and five tiers in the main chamber.

On the north wall of the antechamber is a portrait of the tomb owner, seated and looking forward. The rectangular stone slab below this portrait appears to have been placed there as an altar for incense and other items used in ancestral rituals. In a mural on a wall to the right of the tomb owner's portrait, the governors of the 13 counties of Youzhou[53] are depicted in two horizontal rows, their heads slightly bowed as if about to give a report to him. Beside each governor is the official title he held. On the east wall is a mural depicting the Buddhist ritual of offering seven treasures.[54] The phrase "this man is the governor of Zhongli"[55] is written next to one of the figures participating in the ritual.

Although smaller than Anak Tomb No. 3 in North Korea, this tomb also features a processional scene in a similar arrangement, starting from the south wall of the antechamber and extending to the

---

53 幽州

54 七寶供養

55 此人重裏都督

east wall. The procession proceeds in four horizontal rows, so that all the figures can be easily identified. The owner of the tomb is in the second row, riding a chariot. His chariot is followed by another drawn by oxen and accompanied by maids, but its passenger remains invisible. The two chariots are also accompanied by mounted figures in front, protecting them.

The vaulted ceiling of the antechamber depicts a hunting scene in the lower half and heavenly beings in the upper half. The east and south ceilings each depict groups of eight hunters on horseback shooting arrows at tigers, deer, and wild boars. Above them are Taoist hermits and the celestial beings of legend, Gyeonu and Jingnyeo, among the sun, moon, and stars. A passage with a mural on one wall depicting a circus performance leads to the main chamber, which has another portrait of the tomb owner on its north wall. This portrait is more faded than the one in the antechamber and has a large blank space to the left of the tomb owner. Who exactly was this man depicted without his wife at his side?

Jin, the Tomb Owner

According to the epitaph written in ink, the man buried in this tomb at Deokheung-ri was Jin of [Jung]gam-ri, Sindo-hyeon. His surname, written before his first name, is illegible. The epitaph lists the titles Jin once held, including Geonwi janggun (建威將軍),[56] Gukso-daehyeong (國小大兄),[57] Jwa janggun (左將軍), Yongyang janggun (龍驤將軍), Governor of Liadong,[58] Special Envoy,[59] Colonel of the East Tribe,[60] and *Governor of Youzhou.* Apart from the Guksodaehyeong, there is no evidence that any of these titles were used in Goguryeo. As a result, Jin's background remains a subject of debate among South Korean, North Korean, Chinese, and Japanese scholars.

Jin passed away at the age of 77 and was buried in the tomb when it was completed on the 25th day of the 12th month, in the 18th year of King Gwanggaeto's reign (408). According to the epitaph, Jin was a follower of Buddhism, and "the Duke of Zhou[61] chose the place, Confucius chose the day, and King Wu[62] chose the time" for his burial. Because the chosen place, date, and time for his burial were all excellent, Jin's descendants could hope to "enjoy wealth for seven generations, multiply, and continue to rise in rank to become king one day." The epitaph notes that the efforts of ten thousand men went into the construction of the tomb, for which oxen and sheep were slaughtered every day until the workers were too full to eat any

56 'janggun (將軍)' means 'General' in Korean.

57 國小大兄, It is estimated to have been the 3rd to 4th grade in Goguryeo's 12 (or 13) grade ranking system.

58 遼東太守

59 使持節

60 東夷校尉

61 周公

62 武王

more meat, rice, or liquor, and a month's worth of soy sauce was prepared for their breakfast. In the end, the epitaph reveals that "it was written for posterity and expresses the hope that visitors to the tomb will never run out."

Did Goguryeo's Rule Extend to Beijing?

The Deokheung-ri Tomb walls are richly decorated with various contents. In addition to the epitaph, there are explanations of the murals written in ink, totaling over 600 characters, which is why the tomb has attracted so much attention since its discovery in 1976. Particular attention has been paid to the information provided by the epitaph, such as the fact that the tomb's owner, Jin, was buried in 408 and that he once served as governor of Youzhou. This information has provided vivid clues about the political, social, and cultural circumstances during the reign of King Gwanggaeto that could not be obtained from other historical sources.

In 1978, two years after the discovery of the tomb, color photographs of the epitaph and some of the murals were released in Japan. At that time, North Korean scholars concluded that the owner of the tomb was a Goguryeo man, originally from Sindo-hyeon, who served as governor of Youzhou under King Gwanggaeto. This raised international attention because Youzhou included present-day Beijing, and it was suggested that Goguryeo had once occupied and ruled northern China. Debates arose as to whether the tomb's owner, Jin, was originally from Goguryeo or a Chinese immigrant, and whether Goguryeo had actually expanded into and established Youzhou Province in the area of present-day Beijing and sent Jin to rule it in the mid-to-late fourth century.

To date, a number of research papers have successfully refined the arguments regarding the identity of the tomb's owner and the extent of Goguryeo's rule. Based on the description that "Gaju was originally Sindo-gun of Goryeo" in "the geography section" of *History of Goryeo*,[63] North Korean scholars assumed that Jin's hometown of Sindo-hyeon was located in the area of Unjeon (雲田) and Bakcheon (博川) counties in Pyeonganbuk-do. They also inferred the name of the 'gun' as Mirun (密雲), the former name of Yeongbyeon (寧邊). Their conclusion is that Jin came from Goguryeo and that all the titles he held were given to him by Goguryeo. This would indicate that the ruling system of Goguryeo had settled down considerably between the late fourth and early fifth centuries. Furthermore, the fact that Jin served as governor of Youzhou would suggest that Goguryeo at one point extended its rule over a vast area, from the Liao River basin past the Great Wall through northern Hebei-sheng to the northern part of Shanxi-sheng. These conclusions have been challenged by South

63 『高麗史』「地理志」

Korean, Chinese, and Japanese scholars. North Korean scholars have conducted further studies to support their conclusions, but the conclusions have not changed fundamentally. These conclusions are reflected in North Korean history books such as *The Comprehensive History of Korea*[64] and Volume 3 of *The General History of Korea*.[65]

On the other hand, many South Korean, Chinese, and Japanese scholars have pointed to Xindu County[66] in Hebei-sheng as Jin's hometown, based on the fact that there was a town called Xindu in Anping County (安平國), Jizhou (冀州), according to the first volume of the geography section of the *Book of Jin*.[67] It has been suggested that Jin was a political immigrant from China who received the title of Guksodaehyeong from a Goguryeo king.

Scholars have supported this counterargument based on the fact that the contents of Jin's epitaph are completely different from those in Moduru's tomb, and that the titles listed in Jin's epitaph, except for Guksodaehyeong, seem unrelated to Goguryeo. It has not been confirmed whether the title "janggun" was used in Goguryeo, let alone in such a variety of applications. Of the eight titles mentioned in the epitaph, Geonwi janggun, Guksodaehyeong, Jwa janggun, and Yongyang janggun indicate ranks, while Governor of Liadong, Special Envoy,

64 『朝鮮通史』

65 『朝鮮全史』

66 信都縣

67 『晉書』

Colonel of the East Tribe, and Governor of Yuju indicate government positions. Some believe that all ranks or positions listed after Gukso-daehyeong were self-claimed, and disagree with the suggestion that Youzhou was once occupied and ruled by Goguryeo.

These counterarguments show that there are several questions that North Korean scholars need to answer in order to defend their conclusions: For example, would King Sosurim (r. 371–384), who suddenly ascended to the throne when King Gogukwon died from an arrow shot by Baekje troops, have been able to rise above the chaotic circumstances of the time to invade and seize control of Beijing and send an official to govern that area? And if such detailed subdivisions of the name "janggun" were actually used in Goguryeo, why are they never mentioned in any of the surviving historical records? North Korean scholars must answer these questions.

A Clue from Gyeonu and Jingnyeo?

The portrait of the tomb owner at Deokheung-ri is similar to those at Anak Tomb No. 3 and Yuantaizi (袁台子村) Tomb in Chaoyang (朝阳市). Jin is seated upright, wearing three layers of patterned silk robes and a white or blue silk hat,[68] and holding a feather fan in

68 白羅冠, 青羅冠

Gyeonu and Jingnyeo in the Mural Tombs in Deokheung-ri, Goguryeo

one hand as he gazes ahead. He is surrounded by men and women waiting on him. The face, with its crescent-shaped brows and square but soft jawline, seems to have been drawn to resemble Jin's as much as possible, and is more graceful than the portrait in the Yuantaizi tomb. He appears to be shorter than the owner of Anak Tomb No. 3, who has a longer, stouter face. Although Jin died at 77, much older than average, he was depicted as an imposing middle-aged man in his forties to fifties, like the portraits in other tombs. It might have been customary to portray tomb owners as they looked in the prime of their lives.

The most unusual feature of the Deokheung-ri murals is the absence of a portrait of the tomb owner's wife. According to an expert on Goguryeo murals, possible reasons are that the painter could not remember the woman's face or that the man did not have a wife. In an era before cameras, there would have been no way for the painter to know the appearance of the tomb owner's wife if she had died long before her husband without leaving a portrait of her to serve as a reference. However, it is unlikely that Jin had no wife at all. If he didn't, it would have been more natural to leave no room for her portrait at all. Moreover, the wishes for Jin's descendants written inside the tomb suggest that he definitely had a wife. If she died so much earlier than him that her portrait could not be drawn inside her husband's tomb, she must have been buried elsewhere. But why couldn't she be buried with her husband?

What if Jin, when he commissioned the murals for his own tomb, asked that the space next to his portrait be left blank because he didn't know whether his wife was dead or alive? By the time Jin emigrated to Goguryeo, the Earlier Yan dynasty had taken control of northeastern China, including the areas along the Liao River, and was at war with the Eastern Jin (317–420) and the Earlier Qin (351–394). After declaring himself emperor, the ruler of Earlier Yan decided to attack Goguryeo to secure the rear of his empire. However, a rebellion broke out in Earlier Yan, and some of those who lost in the ensuing political battle sought asylum in Goguryeo. Earlier Yan eventually collapsed under the attacks of Earlier Qin. The circumstances of Jin's emigration remain unknown, but with developments unfolding so rapidly, he could have fled to Goguryeo in a hurry with no guarantee of survival. Could he have been in a situation where he was unable to take his wife and children with him, or was forced to leave only his wife behind? There is no way of knowing, but could it be that he missed his wife so much that he left a blank space next to his portrait in the mural of the main chamber? Perhaps Gyeonu and Jingnyeo, the couple who according to legend could only meet once a year, were painted on the ceiling of the antechamber to express Jin's desperate hope of one day being reunited with his long-lost wife.

5.
A Hero or a Traitor?: Yeon Gaesomun

Playing the Villain?

Yeon Gaesomun frequently appeared in popular operas of the Qing Dynasty. With his terrifying face painted in blue, he was usually one of the most feared characters in any story. He was no ordinary villain either, as he was able to threaten and drive Emperor Taizong of Tang (r. 626–649) into a cul-de-sac with no escape. The hero who saves the Tang from Yeon Gaesomun in the operas turns out to be Xue Rengui (614–683). But although the actual Xue Rengui fought well in the war between the Tang and Goguryeo, there is no mention in the official histories that he saved the emperor's life. Nor was his role significant enough to create a rivalry between him and Yeon Gaesomun. Nevertheless, despite being a member of a northern minority aristocrats, Xue Rengui made significant contributions to the Tang's campaign against Goguryeo. Perhaps he was portrayed as such a great hero because he rose through the ranks as the Tang non-Han Chinese by helping the Tang fight Yeon Gaesomun, an internationally known villain. He became a symbol of hope for both the helpless Tang people and the Qing nobles.

Gaesomun's Goguryeo also appeared frequently in Chinese novels popular during the Ming and Qing dynasties. The fact that he appeared as a symbolic villain in stories more than a thousand years after the actual events shows what a remarkable figure he was. Among Korean historical figures, Yeon Gaesomun has probably been talked about for the longest time and most frequently by Chinese people. In novels, plays and operas, he remains a perennial red-clad villain, while his white-clad counterpart, Xue Rengui, is always portrayed as a heroic figure.

According to his biography in the *History of the Three Kingdoms*, Yeon Gaesomun always carried five swords with him, and every time he went for a ride, he would make someone crouch down so that he could step on his back to mount his house. Whenever he went out, he was accompanied by his men marching in a majestic procession so that people who saw them coming would run into the valleys or jump into pits to hide. These details all suggest that he was a ruthless, ferocious personality.

However, the biography also states that he had a "dignified bearing," implying that he had a magnanimous personality and a sturdy build. Other historical records about Yeon Gaesomun are not very favorable. He was, after all, a man who seized power through a coup d'état that killed his king and nearly 100 high-ranking nobles, and then held on to power for nearly two decades. Anyone who had not met him in person would have thought he was a brutal tyrant and believed his previously described brash behavior.

Born with a Silver Spoon

Yeon Gaesomun was the son of Yeon Taejo (淵胎祚) and the grandson of Yeon Jayu (淵子遊). However, his surname is recorded as Cheon (泉)[69] in Chinese historical records and in the epitaphs of his sons Nam-saeng and Nam-san and his grandson Heon-seong. This is because the first name of the founder of the Tang Dynasty was Yuan (淵)[70] and in order to avoid using the same character in his family name, Yeon Namsaeng chose a character with a similar meaning to use as his surname. According to biography number 145 in volume 220 of the *New Book of Tang*[71] on Goguryeo, it was said that he deceived the world and the people by claiming to be born of water. The

69 The Chinese character '泉' means 'a spring.'

70 The Chinese character '淵' means 'deep water.'

71 *Xin Tangshu* (『新唐書』)

same claim is made in the epitaph of Yeon Gaesomun's son, Yeon Nam-saeng, which states that the family came from a natural spring and entrusted themselves to God.

The connection between water and ancestors is a familiar theme in East Asian myths and folktales. Lady Yuhwa, deified in Goguryeo until that kingdom fell, was known as the daughter of Habaek, the River God. Inspired by the Chinese character jeong (井, meaning a well) inscribed on the bottom of the bronze bowl excavated from the Houchong Tomb (壺杅塚) in Gyeongju, Korea, a modern Korean author named In-ho Choi hypothesized that King Gwanggaeto may have used the same character to mark his army's flag. Although King Gwanggaeto lived in a different century, the fact that Yeon Gaesomun and his family's association with water was widely known suggests that they placed an emphasis on being regarded as divinity. Of course, it is impossible to know whether the story was spread by the family itself or by others who thought it worthy of his status. The latter seems more plausible, since the epitaph of Yeon Nam-saeng discovered in Luoyang mentions the connection of his ancestors with the founder of Goguryeo, Jumong. However, there is no way to be certain.

It seems certain that Yeon Gaesomun was born with a silver spoon in his mouth. His father, Yeon Taejo, came from a leading family in the east and had served as Daedaero,[72] one of the highest posi-

72 大對盧

tions in the Goguryeo government. According to the *Book of Zhou*,[73] each Daedaero served for three years. If there was no consensus on who should serve next, the candidates would resort to violence, and whoever won would become the new Daedaero. Instead of interfering in this process, the king was expected to remain in his palace and wait for a decision to be made. This suggests that by the late Goguryeo period, the king's authority had weakened to the point where nobles were commanding their own armies. While we cannot be sure whether the position of Daedaero was still held by force in Yeon Taejo's time, his service in the position suggests that his family's power was based on its military might.

Depending on the source, Yeon Taejo is sometimes referred to as the Dongbudaein, or the leader of the East, and sometimes as the Seobudaein, or the leader of the West. However, considering a variety of circumstances, scholars tend to assume the former.

After his father's death, Yeon Gaesomun attempted to inherit his father's rank of Dongbudaein, but was opposed by nobles who saw flaws in his character. Even in its later years, Goguryeo maintained the tradition of deciding important state matters through a council of nobles, so that even the king could not make arbitrary decisions. However, it was still a monarchy, which meant that the king also had a say in whether the son of an influential noble could inherit his

73 『周書』

father's rank. In the case of Yeon Gaesomun, both the king and the nobles objected his inheritance of the title of Dongbudaein.

At that time, Goguryeo was ruled by King Yeongnyu (r. 618–642), who, as Prince Geonmu, is described as having led five million troops to defend Pyongyang Castle when it was attacked by Sui forces. King Yeongnyu and the nobles of Goguryeo had been wary of Yeon Gaesomun's potential for seizing power from the beginning, suggesting that Yeon Gaesomun had been conspicuous since his early years. He had no choice but to remain humble and beg the nobles to allow him to inherit the title of Dongbudaein. He even promised to renounce the title at any time if they demanded it for any wrongdoing he might commit. This gave the nobles who disapproved of him no reason to oppose him. Eventually, he was able to become Dongbudaein and reclaim the troops and purse strings that his father had controlled in the east.

Ruthless Ascent to the Top

Yeon Gaesomun may have promised to give up his title at any time if he committed any wrongdoings, but his underlying temperament would never change. Judging from the fact that the king and the nobles tried to get rid of him after he entered the political scene as Dongbudaein, he must have been uncompromising whenever his views differed from those of others in dealing with domestic and foreign policy issues or in setting policy directions. For example, after King Yeongnyu ascended the throne, Goguryeo adopted a submissive attitude toward the Tang and even offered a sensitive fief map if necessary to maintain friendly relations with them. This foreign policy may have caused strife between the King's followers and Yeon Gaesomun.

Meanwhile, Yeon Gaesomun expanded his own private army and built his power by bringing in other Generals who agreed with his ideas. The more power he gained, the more doubt and fear he instilled in his opponents. In response, King Yeongnyu put Yeon Gaesomun in charge of the construction of the Wall of Thousand-ri to send him to the frontier and conspired with other nobles to eliminate him.

However, Yeon Gaesomun caught wind of their plot. In 642, under the pretext of conducting a military inspection of the troops in the region, he invited about one hundred nobles who opposed him to a place south of Pyongyang Castle. When they arrived, he ordered them all to be killed. The biography of Yeon Gaesomun in the *History of the Three Kingdoms* describes this incident as follows.

> "Somun (Yeon Gaesomun) summoned all the troops in his region and prepared heaps of food and drink in front of the south wall of the castle, as if preparing for a military inspection, and invited many officials to join him. When the guests, who numbered nearly a hundred men, arrived, he killed them all. Then he ran to the palace and killed the king, cutting him

into pieces and throwing them into a ditch. He placed Jang (藏), the son of the king's younger brother, on the throne and took the title of Mangniji, a position equivalent to holding the both positions of Minister of War[74] and Director of the Secretariat[75] in the Tang China. After that, he issued orders to near and far of the country to handle state affairs as he saw fit, which made him appear quite dignified."

Yeon Gaesomun couldn't just wait and do nothing, so he had to take preemptive strike by killing the king and the officials. Historical sources do not go into detail about how brutal and cruel Yeon Gaesomun was. The following description comes after the massacre of the king and noble officials and serves as a testament to the absolute power Yeon Gaesomun wielded during King Bojang's reign (642–668), but whether he behaved the same way before the massacre remains unknown:

"Whenever he mounted or dismounted a horse, he always made a noble General crouch on the ground and stepped on the man's back. Whenever he went out, he had his troops go ahead of him. The man at the front would give a long shout to alert the people, who would then run off into a valley or a pit."

74 兵部尙書

75 中書令

The above describes his character, but only after he took full power after the murder of the king. We have no information about what he was like before. Even though Yeon Gaesomun had placed a new king on the throne and taken complete control of the court, the nobles who were sent to areas outside the capital or who served as local officials in their respective hometowns were still out of his reach. Those nobles were not only in charge of local administration, but also had military command authority. If Yeon Gaesomun failed to deal with them properly, there was a possibility that they would revolt to punish him for murdering their king. Yeon Gaesomun began to reach out to these local officials, and most of them swore allegiance to him. One exception was the lord of Ansi Fortress,[76] who refused to submit. However, he was unable to rebel on his own, and with the Tang China's movements growing increasingly suspicious, Yeon Gaesomun compromised to allow him to retain his position for the time being. The political chaos in the capital spread to the Han River and caused the monk Hyeryang Beopsa to defect to Silla, a sign that Goguryeo would remain unstable for some time.

---

76 安市城

Was Yeon Gaesomun a Defender of Independence?

Yeon Gaesomun has often been the subject of historians' evaluations because his personal fate was tied to the tumultuous fate of Goguryeo. His moves have been compared to those of his rivals or figures who made contrasting decisions, such as the Tang Emperor Taizong, King Yeongnyu, and Kim Chun-chu of Silla (603–661).

Emperor Taizong brought all the states and political opponents around him to their knees except for Goguryeo. Although he went to war against Goguryeo several times, he only exhausted the Tang's resources without succeeding in conquering Goguryeo. One of his last words to his descendants, apparently, was never to attack Goguryeo again. What would have annoyed the emperor even more is that after his death, stories about him, Yeon Gaesomun, and Xue Rengui were passed on to the Chinese people for a long time. Although Emperor Taizong never met or fought against Yeon Gaesomun in real life, not only do the two meet in novels and plays, but the Emperor ends up being chased helplessly by Yeon Gaesomun until Xue Rengui comes to his rescue. In any case, although Emperor Taizong became the Emperor Khan of Heaven[77] who ruled the central plains and surrounding nomadic regions, he ultimately failed to bring Goguryeo to its knees.

King Yeongnyu primarily tried to maintain friendly relations

---

77 皇帝天可汗

with the Tang. Yeon Gaesomun, on the other hand, is said to have taken a hard line against the Tang. For this reason, Shin Chae-ho, a Korean independence activist and historian, regarded him as a hero who increased the autonomy of the Koreans. To Shin, King Yeong-nyu was a shameful sycophant. His comparison of Yeon Gaesomun and Kim Chun-chu was no different. Some historians have concluded that Kim Chun-chu emerged victorious in history through realistic, flexible diplomacy. He knew when to compromise and when to make bold moves. Yeon Gaesomun, on the other hand, is said to have pursued an uncompromising, rigid policy that led Goguryeo down the path to collapse. Contrastingly, though, Shin Chae-ho regarded Kim Chun-chu as a servile opportunist, but viewed Yeon Gaesomun as a national hero and defender of autonomy who stood up to the great Tang Empire who had unified the central plains of China.

It is certainly true that Gaesomun refused to submit to the Tang's great power and fought to the end to preserve Goguryeo's independence and autonomy. But what about the rest of his actions and policies? What credit can be given to a man who ruthlessly murdered his own king and numerous noble officials, appointed himself Mangniji, and then promoted himself to Great Mangniji,[78] before bequeathing his title to his incompetent children, all of which contributed to the ultimate collapse of Goguryeo?

---

78 大莫離支, It is today's prime minister.

"What Ifs" in History

It is often said that there are no "what ifs" in history. It is useless to dwell on what might have been, and more importantly, such an unscientific approach to the study of history should be discouraged. However, applying this approach to the case of Yeon Gaesomun–even if it is generally discouraged among academics–may help us to look at his actions from a completely different historical perspective. Emperor Taizong always rationalized the Tang's attacks on Goguryeo by citing the phrase "mourning the people and punishing the guilty"[79] in his declarations of war to claim that he was sending troops to punish Yeon Gaesomun for murdering the king. But what if Gaesomun had not committed treason? What if he had not murdered King Yeongnyu?

As mentioned above, King Yeongnyu was a hero who had defended Pyongyang Castle during the Goguryeo-Sui War several years ago. However, after he ascended the throne, his basic attitude toward the Tang was to maintain peace. He never failed to send envoys to pay tribute to the Tang. On the seventh month of 626, when the Tang demanded that Goguryeo reconcile with Baekje and Silla (57–935 BCE), King Yeongnyu sent a message of apology to the emperor and agreed to make a treaty with Silla. When the Tang defeated the Turks

79 弔民伐罪, this Chinese phrase expresses the idea of seeking justice for the people by punishing those who have committed crimes or wrongdoings.

in 628, the king sent a delegation to congratulate the Tang and offer the sensitive map of Goguryeo territory. In 629, Silla captured the Goguryeo stronghold of Nangbi Castle, but King Yeongnyu took no action to follow the Tang's advice to reconcile with Silla and Baekje. Even when the Tang envoys destroyed a monument built to celebrate Goguryeo's victory over the Sui (581–618), King Yeongnyu let the matter rest. The Goguryeo king thus worked hard to maintain friendly relations with the Tang, but their demands continued to grow.

At this point, it seems necessary to review who Emperor Taizong was. Although he was a hero who contributed greatly to the founding of the Tang Empire, Taizong was not an heir to the throne. He had seized it only through a coup d'état staged at Xuanwu Gate,[80] where he ruthlessly murdered his two brothers, including Crown Prince Li Jiancheng,[81] and soon after forced his father to abdicate. His legitimacy was therefore tainted, as was that of the Sui Emperor Yangdi (r. 604–618), who launched military campaigns against Goguryeo. Some scholars have even suggested that Emperor Taizong sought to conquer Goguryeo in order to overcome the handicap of his lack of legitimacy.

Once on the throne, Emperor Taizong worked swiftly to turn numerous Northeast Asian powers into the Tang vassals. When the Heishu Mohe[82] came under his control in 628, Emperor Taizong estab-

80 玄武門之變

81 建成太子 (李建成)

82 黑水靺鞨

lished a jimi (羈縻)[83] prefecture called Yanzhou (燕州) in their land. In the same year, the Khitans[84] also surrendered to the Tang. In 629, the Tang began negotiations with the Shiwei (室韋). Through the Khitans, the Tang also persuaded the Xi (奚) and the Shi (霫) to surrender. In the third month of 630, the Tang captured alive Illig Qaghan (頡利可汗) of the Eastern Turkic Khaganate, and all the nomadic tribal leaders of the steppes surrounding China except Goguryeo fell on their knees before him, calling him Emperor Taizong "Tengri Khagan" (天可汗, Khan of Heaven). He had finally become the emperor who had unified the Jungwon and the khan with control over the surrounding areas. The only independent state left around him was Goguryeo - and Goguryeo's influence over the nomads had gradually waned as the Tang gained control over the Mohe, the Khitans, and the Shiwei.

In the sixth month of 643, the Tang envoy named Deng Su (鄧素) visited Goguryeo. Upon his return, he advised Emperor Taizong to reinforce the troops stationed at Huaiyuanzhen (懷遠鎭), as Goguryeo had been fortifying its borders since Yeon Gaesomun's rise to power. The inauguration of Goguryeo King Bojang was brought up at the the Tang royal court, leading to discussions of war. Emperor Taizong and Chief Minister Zhangsun Wuji (長孫無忌, 594–659) debated whether to

83 羈縻, This expression in Chinese means that "to hold the reins loosely without cutting off the relationship." It referred to a policy of control or governance used by a dominant state over a weaker state or tribe.

84 契丹

mobilize the Khitans and Mohe to attack Goguryeo or to wait until Goguryeo might let down its guard. These discussions about conquering Goguryeo took place despite the fact that the Tang had introduced Taoism to Goguryeo at Goguryeo's request in the third month of 643 and had invested King Bojang a few months later in the sixth month of that year.

In the first month of 644, Xiangli Xuanjiang (相里玄奬) arrived in Goguryeo as a the Tang envoy. He brought a message from Emperor Taizong, which included a warning that the Tang would subjugate Goguryeo if it did not desist from military action against Silla. Xiangli Xuanjiang repeated the emperor's warning when he met with Yeon Gaesomun, who had just returned from attacking Silla with his own troops. He made it clear that Goguryeo had no intention of complying with the Tang request. It would be easy to conclude that Goguryeo refused to change its belligerent attitude toward Silla and Baekje, even though the Tang demanded that Goguryeo make a peace treaty with Silla and Baekje for the sake of regional peace and stability.

However, a closer look at Xiangli Xuanjiang's identity reveals that such a conclusion would be premature. Xiangli Xuanjiang was a level 6 minor official, the lowest rank among the envoys sent abroad by the emperor. Moreover, according to a research paper, his position at the Court of Imperial Granaries[85] had nothing to do with Gogu-

85 司農寺

ryeo. The same paper concluded that Emperor Taizong had no expectations when he sent Xiangli Xuanjiang to Goguryeo, but only sent him to make a political excuse to justify a war he planned to launch. Yeon Gaesomun may have seen through the Tang Emperor's intention, so he brought up the Goguryeo-Sui war while declaring that Goguryeo would make its own moves. In the seventh month of 644, after Xiangli Xuanjiang returned, Emperor Taizong declared that the Tang would subjugate Goguryeo, sending Jiang Yan (蔣儼) as an envoy to Goguryeo. At that time, everyone was afraid and reluctant to undertake this mission. Actually, Jiang Yan went through hardships, including being imprisoned in a cave by Yeon Gaesomun. Yeon Gaesomun may have sensed that he was sent to gather information about Goguryeo before the war.

It is interesting to note that even as tensions between the two states were rising, Goguryeo sent platinum as an offering to the Tang along with 50 officials to serve as imperial guards[86] at the Tang's request. For someone from Goguryeo to serve as an imperial guard was to be a political hostage. Indeed, the Goguryeo officials were imprisoned upon their arrival in the Tang. Of course, they would have known this would happen if they went, and Yeon Gaesomun would have expected it as well when he sent them. While it remains uncertain whether Goguryeo made these gestures as a last resort to prevent

86 宿衛

war, or in an attempt to gain intelligence on the Tang's internal situation, the war had already begun.

Like King Yeongyang (r. 590–618) before him, Yeon Gaesomun launched a blitz attack against the Liaoxi (遼西) before the Tang forces could move in. It is generally believed that the attack was aimed at the troops of other ethnic groups under the command of the Liaoxi lord, such as the Khitans or the Xi, as they were likely to be placed at the front of the Tang forces. Another theory is that the attack was carried out to cut off supplies to Liaoxi in case the Tang forces decided to launch a full-scale attack on the Liaodong region and engage in a prolonged war.

Considering all these circumstances, we can assume that Emperor Taizong, in his eagerness to dominate the "world," would not let Goguryeo remain under its own rule. Even if Yeon Gaesomun had not rebelled and King Yeongnyu had remained on the throne, it is doubtful that Goguryeo would have maintained its independence.

This brings us to the second "what if." What if Yeon Gaesomun had acceded to the request of Kim Chun-chu of Silla when he came to ask for military reinforcements, or had formed an alliance with Silla to restore their relationship to that of friendly neighbors?

Having lost his daughter and son-in-law to Baekje during the battle at Daeyas Fortress, Kim Chun-chu came to Goguryeo shortly after Gaesomun's coup to ask for military alliance with Silla. He met with King Bojang and Yeon Gaesomun, who both said that they could not grant his request unless Silla returned Mamok-hyeon and the land north of the Juk Peak that Silla had conquered during the Goguryeo-Sui War.

Kim Chun-chu said that this was impossible because he did not have the authority to make such a decision, and Yeon Gaesomun detained him. While Kim Chun-chu was racking his brains to find a way out, a Goguryeo nobleman named Seon Do-hae came and told him the *Tale of the Hare*.[87] Inspired by this story, Kim Chun-chu promised the Goguryeo king and Yeon Gaesomun that he would return to Silla and convince the Silla king to return what had apparently been Goguryeo territory. Of course, this promise was nothing more than a ploy to get himself released.

Once out of Goguryeo, Kim Chun-chu went to the Tang to ask for reinforcements, which eventually led to an alliance between the Tang and Silla. With the help of the Tang, Silla was able to free itself from the threat of Baekje and defeat it. Furthermore, with Silla's help, the Tang could continue to engage in war against Goguryeo without worrying about supplies and finally achieve a victory after many failed attempts in the past. But would history have turned out differently if Goguryeo had allied itself with Silla?

During the reign of King Gwanggaeto, Goguryeo had responded to a request for military assistance from King Naemul (r. 356–402) and

87 『토끼전』, An old fable about a trapped rabbit outsmarting a turtle and escaping from difficulty.

helped Silla drive out the Japanese forces that had penetrated as far as Seorabeol (modern-day Gyeong-ju). This eventually allowed Silla to destroy and take over the state of Geumgwan Gaya, the neighboring southern state. After that, Goguryeo called Silla its vassal. By the time of King Jangsu, the relationship between the two states had improved to one of fraternity, although Goguryeo still bestowed official Goguryeo robes on the Silla king and his court officials. By the mid-to-late 5th century, however, Silla had emerged from Goguryeo's shadow, forming an alliance with Baekje, seizing Goguryeo territory along the east coast, and advancing northward. In the central part of the Korean peninsula, Silla allied with Baekje to advance beyond Juk Peak and seize territory in the Han River basin.

Although Goguryeo and Silla were neighbors who had developed a love-hate relationship over the years, why did Yeon Gaesomun refused to help Silla and made such an unrealistic demand for the return of lost lands? At that time, Yeon Gaesomun had yet to gain a firm grip on the affairs of state. In addition, Goguryeo had to focus all its efforts on preparing for attacks from the Tang, including the construction of the Wall of Thousand-ri, which had begun during the reign of King Yeongnyu. It could not afford to send troops to help Silla. In addition, Silla had taken land from Goguryeo while it was busy defending itself against Sui attacks. Having risen to power by assassinating the king, Yeon Gaesomun had to win the hearts of the people, and the best way to do so was to regain the lost territory and bring Silla and Baekje under Goguryeo's control. Joining forces with Silla to attack Baekje was never an option in Yeon Gaesomun's mind.

The same could be said of Silla. Although Silla was in a dire situation due to its defeat by Baekje, it had no intention of becoming a vassal or little brother to Goguryeo again. The past was the past, and there was no going back. Even if the hands of a clock could be turned back, Yeon Gaesomun and Kim Chun-chu would have made the same decisions. Looking at this "what if" scenario only leads to the conclusion that nothing would have changed. In other words, even though Yeon Gaesomun's refusal led to an alliance between Silla and the Tang that would eventually lead to the fall of Goguryeo, the decisions that Yeon Gaesomun and Kim Chun-chu made in their respective situations were inevitable.

Although the fall of Goguryeo came after Yeon Gaesomun's death, he was responsible for it to some extent. After his death, his sons split up their father's powers and fought among themselves. One of them, Nam-saeng who was defeated by his brothers, went to the Tang with his son Heon-seong to serve as the leader of the Tang forces and later attacked Goguryeo, causing the collapse of the country. Yeon Gaesomun is also responsible for this. After staging his coup, he appointed himself Mangniji, and as tensions between Goguryeo and the Tang grew, he created a new position for himself, Great Mangniji, to oversee both state and military affairs. He also began promoting his sons early in order to pass on his power to them. When

Emperor Taizong personally led the Tang troops to attack Goguryeo, Yeon Gaesomun sent his son Nam-saeng to stop them at the mouth of the Aprok River. However, Nam-saeng was utterly defeated and barely escaped alive. Yeon Gaesomun should have realized that Nam-saeng did not have what it takes to be a leader and abandoned the idea of passing his title on to him. Unfortunately, like many parents, Yeon Gaesomun failed to keep a level head when it came to his sons. On his deathbed, he summoned Nam-saeng and other sons to ask them to stick together and move forward. Perhaps he had already sensed signs of division among them, but that did not stop him from entrusting them with important positions responsible for the security of Goguryeo.

In a way, his self-appointment as Mangniji and his elevation to Great Mangniji could be justified as a means of stabilizing the administration of state affairs and concentrating power to enable quick responses to the Tang's aggressive threats. Nevertheless, Yeon Gaesomun was the one who placed his relatives and those close to him in positions of power, resulting in a schism between his sons that brought down an entire kingdom in the blink of an eye. Yeon Gaesomun can also be blamed for maintaining such a rigid stance against the Tang, Silla, and Baekje, leading to war when a more flexible response would have been more effective.

Should he then be considered a hero in the eyes of history, or a traitor who brought down a kingdom? Although the answer to this question remains unclear, one cannot help but think that he seems to have been helplessly swept along by the tide of history, just like so many others.

6.
Doesn't the Apple Fall Too Far from the Tree?: Yeon Gaesomun's Descendants

Around 2005, a heated debate erupted in the Republic of Korea over the issue of children of some high-ranking officials having foreign citizenship. Some thought that changing one's nationality does not necessarily mean losing love for the motherland. There were some who argued that having citizenship of other countries and working to benefit Korea would be advantageous, as it would make it easier to work outside the country. Some also argued that giving up South Korean citizenship for American citizenship should not be a problem in this global age. They all made arguments that seemed convincing, but public opinion on changing one's citizenship remained negative. Most Koreans who lacked money and power resented these people's change of citizenship because it allowed them to enjoy the privileges of living in Korea without having to fulfill the obligations imposed on other Korean citizens. Even though nearly two decades have passed since then, the issue still comes up for debate during inspection of government officials in Korea.

However, there have always been cases of people changing their nationality. More precisely, people have left their homelands throughout history. Before modern times, almost no one lived in the motherland after changing his or her nationality. People left their homelands for various reasons: to pursue greater dreams, to escape poverty, or to work for the restoration of nations lost to colonial rule. Some people had left just before their countries collapsed. Cheon Heon-seong was one of them.

Cheon Heon-seong was none other than the son of Cheon Nam-saeng and the grandson of the famous Yeon Gaesomun. As explained earlier, the sons and grandsons of Yeon Gaesomun changed their family name to Cheon to avoid a name with a pronunciation similar to the Tang founder's first name, Yuan. This name change was inevitable even after death because they had placed their fate in the hands of the Tang. Therefore, the names Cheon Nam-saeng and Cheon Heon-seong were used even in their epitaphs and in the biographies of the *New Book of the Tang*.

Yeon Gaesomun's family were rising aristocrats in the late Goguryeo period, and the progenitor of the family was said to have been born from water. In ancient times, many kings and powerful nobles had their own myths about the birth of the progenitor to emphasize the sanctity of the family. However, not everyone could claim to have descended from a water god. The Yeon family could do so because they were at the pinnacle of power in late Goguryeo. The myth of the Yeon family's birth thus suggests that their prestige was close to that of the founder of Goguryeo, Jumong, whose parents were said to be Haemosu, the son of Sky God, and Lady Yuhwa, the daughter of River God Habaek.

Nam-saeng's epitaph states that he enjoyed prestige thanks to his ancestors. Meanwhile, Heon-seong's epitaph states that his grandfather, Daejo (大祚), controlled Goguryeo's armed forces as Mangniji and had influence as the head of the Five Bu (部) administrative system, which extended to the Three Han confederations.[88] The biography of Yeon Gaesomun in the *History of the Three Kingdoms* only mentions that his father held the title of Dongbudaein.

Thus, the family seems to have moved to the center of power during the time of Yeon Gaesomun's father. Since the myth of the family's birth was known in the Tumen River valley region, prominent families from that area seem to have been able to move to the center of the political scene during the sixth and seventh centuries. Considering Yeon Gaesomun's powerful status at that time, it seems highly plausible that the water myth was created at that time.

However, the family name had to be changed to Cheon when

---

88 三韓

Yeon Gaesomun's son inherited his title. With the decline of the family's status, the water described in the myth was reduced from a pond to a spring. Unlike his father, who defended Goguryeo against massive Sui attacks and defeated the army of Emperor Taizong of the Tang, Nam-saeng and his son played a major role in the collapse of Goguryeo.

Cheon Heon-seong was born in 650, when his grandfather Yeon Gaesomun was at the peak of his power. As the grandson of the most powerful man in Goguryeo, Heon-seong was given the rank of Seonin[89] at the age of nine. Then, in 666, the year Heon-seong turned sixteen, his grandfather died and his father Nam-saeng inherited the title of Mangniji. Nam-saeng then set out on an inspection tour of districts outside the capital, with Heon-seong accompanying his father. But after they left Pyongyang Castle, something happened that changed the fate of both Heon-seong and Goguryeo forever. Nam-saeng's brothers Nam-geon (男建) and Nam-san (男産) betrayed their brother and staged a coup. Having lost the power struggle to his brothers, Nam-saeng was unable to return to Pyongyang. He sat down with his faction to discuss their next move, but they had difficulty coming to a conclusion. That's when Heon-seong suggested that they should better go to Goguryeo's second capital at Gungnae Fortress (in present-day Ji'an, Jilin-sheng).

---

89 先人, the 13th-ranked official position among the 14 administrative ranks of Goguryeo.

The nobles of Gungnae Fortress had been dissatisfied with the nobles of Pyongyang as their status was weakened after the capital had been transferred to Pyongyang. Judging from the huge tombs with exquisite murals left in the area, these nobles continued to enjoy considerable power and wealth for a long time even after the transfer of the capital. However, their dissatisfaction with their counterparts in Pyongyang had hardly subsided. In fact, in 557, a General named Gan Ju-ri (干朱理) near Gungnae revolted at Hwando Fortress. Therefore, Heon-seong hoped to ride on the back of the discontent of the Gungnae Fortress nobles to regain power. However, contrary to his expectations, not all of the nobles of Gungnae Fortress were willing to fully support Heon-seong and his father. Nam-saeng and Heon-seong had recently gained power through Yeon Gaesomun's coup so the nobles of Gungnae Fortress who had maintained their status since the founding of the Goguryeo were not in favor of them. These nobles were also reluctant because their military power was inferior to that of Pyongyang Castle.

When things did not go as planned, Nam-saeng had to come up with an alternative plan. Heon-seong suggested that they should go to the Tang, plead their case, and ask for troops to help attack his uncles. Nam-saeng had no better idea, so he sent his 16-year-old son ahead of him and followed with his men. It was the year 666, the 25th year of the king Bojang. Two years later, in 668, Nam-saeng and his men, now leaders of the Tang forces, launched an attack on Pyongyang

Castle, which eventually caused the collapse of Goguryeo.

Nam-saeng and Heon-seong then lived as subjects of the Tang emperor in the capital of the empire, Chang'an. Because they had voluntarily become naturalized as the Tang citizens and contributed greatly to the fall of Goguryeo, they remained close to the emperor as wealthy high-ranking officials. Nam-saeng rose to the position of Tejin (特進), which corresponds to the rank two above literary officer.[90] He also served as Youwei dajiangjun (右衛大將軍), Jianxiao (檢校), Youyu linjun (右羽林軍), Zhangnei gongfeng (仗內供奉), Shangzhuguo (上柱國), and Bianguogong (卞國公), and after his death he was posthumously given the title of Bingzhou dadudu (幷州大都督). Heon-seong, meanwhile, served as Zuowei dajiangjun (左衛大將軍), Youyu linwei shangxia (右羽林衛上下), Shangzhuguo (上柱國), and Bianguogong (卞國公). He was posthumously awarded the title of Youyu linwei dajiangjun (右羽林衛大將軍).[91] They served in close proximity to the emperor supervising the Imperial Household Guard[92] or Palace Guard.[93]

After the fall of Goguryeo, the people who had lost the country emigrated to the Tang through various routes. Nam-saeng and Heon-seong were given high ranks, second only to those of King Bojang and his descendants. In some ways, they wielded more real power

90 正二品 文散官

91 These are high titles in the Tang Empire.

92 宮禁宿衛

93 近衛兵

than King Bojang, who was given only a symbolic, honorary position. Nam-saeng even participated in the government of the Goguryeo immigrants, albeit in a different role from that of King Bojang. In 677, the year after the end of the Silla-Tang War, the Tang granted King Bojang the title of Korean King and Governor-General of Liaodong.[94] The Tang had difficulty in governing the rebellious Goguryeo immigrants, so a puppet state was established in order to control them through King Bojang. To keep an eye on their Goguryeo immigrants, the Tang established a dual system of government. King Bojang would remain as their king, but Nam-saeng, a dedicated pro-Tang official, would be sent there as the Protector-General to Pacify the East (PGPE)[95] to keep King Bojang in check.

King Bojang saw through the Tang's intentions, and when he returned to Liaodong, he attempted to revive Goguryeo by joining forces with the Sumo Mohe,[96] who had once been Goguryeo people. Unfortunately, his plot was discovered and the Tang banished him to Qiongzhou (邛州) in 681. He died the following year, ending his shameful life as a king who had lost his kingdom.

Historical sources do not mention how the Tang learned of King Bojang's plot. However, judging by the Tang's style of government, it seems likely that the PGPE sent word to the central court. Of

---

94 遼東都督

95 安東都護府

96 粟末靺鞨

course, there is no way to be sure of the details, and it is also possible that someone close to King Bojang betrayed him, but what seems most likely is that the PGPE caught wind of the plot beforehand while monitoring the king.

Could Nam-saeng have been the informant? It seems unlikely, since he died of illness in his official residence as the PGPE on the 29th of first month, 679. After leading the enemy forces to destroy his homeland, Nam-saeng died at Sin Fortress in present-day Fushun, Liaoning-sheng, which was once part of Goguryeo. While it may be regrettable for someone to die at the relatively young age of 46, it may also be fortunate that he was gone before he had another chance to betray Goguryeo.

Heon-seong was a most devoted son. When his father Nam-saeng passed away, he stopped eating and drinking out of grief. His epitaph describes how his grandmother went into fasting and prayer to save him. Heonseong had no choice but to consume food again. This suggests that father and son shared a strong bond, perhaps forged as they faced the most dramatic moments of their lives together. From the way he fully supported his son's ideas when he could not decide what to do after being betrayed by his brothers, Nam-saeng obviously had great faith in his son. In retrospect, however, a different picture emerges: an incompetent father who followed the immature advice of his 16-year-old son and led the entire family into a group of traitors, committing an unforgivable sin. When Heon-seong suggested that they ask the Tang for help, Nam-saeng should have considered the case of one of his ancestors, a man named Balgi (發岐), before choosing this irreversible path.

Balgi was the younger brother of King Gogukcheon (故國川王, r. 179–197) and the elder brother of King Sansang (山上王, r. 197–227). After the death of King Gogukcheon, Queen Wu chose his younger brother Yeonu (延優) to succeed him on the throne. Enraged by the queen's decision, Balgi turned to the Chinese warlord Gongsun Du (公孫度) for military aid to rebel against the queen and Yeonu. When the youngest of his brothers, Gyesu (罽須), came to suppress the rebellion, he pleaded with Balgi and advised him to stop, which made Balgi feel so remorseful that he took his own life.

Nam-saeng, on the other hand, brought the Tang troops to Goguryeo to seek revenge on his younger brothers who had betrayed him, and ultimately became an unforgivable failure of a leader who destroyed his homeland and its people. Perhaps his death in what should have been the prime of his life is proof that he was not necessarily comfortable or happy during his lifetime. But what happened to Heon-seong after his death? Since he had placed his fate in the hands of the Tang, the only way for him to survive was to continue to prove his loyalty. So, then, he was called upon to fight for the Tang in countless battles, even while mourning his father's death. It was not a pleasant life for a devoted son.

Most of the Goguryeo people who voluntarily surrendered to the

Tang retained their noble ranks were mobilized by the Tang in wars to conquer other ethnic groups. In fact, this was a time-honored tactic used by many Chinese dynasties throughout history when fighting other ethnic groups. Placing a non-Han Chinese group in the front line to subjugate another non-Han Chinese group was probably a shrewd tactic to protect the Han Chinese. All of the Tang officials originally from Goguryeo were required to fight for the Tang, and since they tended to have excellent military skills, quite a few made outstanding contributions on the battlefields. Cheon Heon-seong was also famous for his military prowess. Empress Wu Zetian (則天武后, r. 690–705) once offered gold coins to the best archers among her subjects and held a vote. When Heon-seong received the most votes, he addressed the empress, saying, "Your Majesty, none of those chosen as the best archers are Han Chinese. I am afraid that the Tang officials will feel humiliated, so I beg you to stop this vote."[97]

As this episode shows, Heon-seong chose his words and actions carefully, as the so-called kuli (酷吏 cruel officials) serving under Empress Wu Zetian's rule made the political scene difficult to navigate. On the plus side, officials were hired fairly based on their abilities, but the downside was that politics was rife with slander and brutal executions. Goguryeo immigrants could have successful careers if they were sufficiently competent and loyal, but they ran the risk of

97 The original expression in Chinese is the following. 陛下擇善射者 然皆非華人 臣恐唐官以射爲恥 不如罷之

being framed and executed for crimes they did not commit. For this reason, Heon-seong did not want to stand out for his military prowess. Nevertheless, his skills and loyalty were recognized enough to allow him to serve the emperor closely. When the Axis of Heaven,[98] a huge copper pillar inscribed with the achievements of Empress Wu Zetian, was erected, he was appointed as the Imperial Envoy of the Axis of Heaven,[99] in charge of procuring the supplies needed for the task, including copper. Unfortunately, this turned out to be his last position. An official named Lai Junchen (來俊臣) demanded a bribe from Heon-seong. When he refused, Lai Junchen framed him, claiming that he was plotting a conspiracy. Heon-seong was finally executed at the age of 42.

Cheon Heon-seong had three sons, Hyeon-eun (玄隱), Hyeon-il (玄逸), and Hyeon-jeong (玄靜), but records only remain about Hyeon-eun, the eldest son. Although the gravestone of Hyeon-eun has not been found, his name is mentioned in the epitaphs of his father, Heon-seong, and the tombstone of his son, Cheon Bi (泉毖), who died prematurely at the age of 22. Cheon Bi's epitaph states that he was a native of Jingzhao (京兆), the capital city of Tang Dynasty.[100] This contrasts with other Goguryeo immigrants' tombstones. The epitaph of Cheon Nam-saeng, a first-generation Goguryeo immigrant, states

98 天樞

99 檢校天樞子來使

100 京兆萬年人

The Ancestral Tombs of the Cheon Nam-saeng's Family

Located in Yeongdu Village, Dongsan, Mengjin County, Luoyang City, China (洛陽市 孟津縣 東山 嶺頭村). In the center is the tomb of Nam-saeng, to the left is the tomb of Cheon Heon-seong, and to the right is the tomb of Cheon Bi. (Photographed in 2006).

The Tomb of Cheon Nam-san

It is located in Yugapachon (劉家坡村), northeast of Luoyang City, China. It stands alone in the middle of a barley field beyond the cornfield, and in this area, it is called "Pyojachong" (豹子塚). (Photographed in 2006).

that he was from Pyongyang Castle and lived in Liaodong County. Based on other epitaphs that mention where the deceased came from and where they lived, Go Ja (高慈) was a Joseon person, Cheon Heon-seong was a descendant of Goguryeo people, Cheon Namsan was a Liaodong person from Joseon, Go Jog-yu (高足酉) was a Liaodong person from Pyongyang, and Go Hyeon (高玄) was a Liaodong person from the Three Han confederations. Among the descendants of the Goguryeo immigrants, Go Jin (高震) and his fourth daughter, and Go Heumdeok (高欽德) were all described as Balhae people in their epitaphs. According to other historical sources, Go Seon-ji (高仙芝), Wang Mojung (王毛仲), Wang Sarye (王思禮), and Yi Jeong-gi (李正己) were all originally from Goguryeo. However, the epitaph of Cheon Bi only mentioned that he is from the capital of the Tang Dynasty.

Since only one generation had passed since the fall of Goguryeo, everyone must have known that Cheon Bi was from Goguryeo and was the grandson of a famous Goguryeo statesman. But why did Cheon Bi's epitaph describe him as a native of the Tang capital and make no mention of his ties to Goguryeo? Could people have forgotten about Goguryeo altogether? That seems unlikely.

Yi Jeong-gi and Go Seon-ji were third-generation immigrants, but historical records still mention that their ancestors came from Goguryeo. Moreover, Go Seon-ji's competitors and political rivals derisively referred to him as a "Goryeo servant." This raises the possibility that Cheon Heon-seong did not mention Goguryeo in his son's epitaph because the family's ties to the fallen kingdom were well known. Or perhaps he wanted to bury with him all they had gone through, along with the remorse they felt as immigrants who had betrayed their homeland.

These considerations are also echoed in the epitaphs of Nam-saeng and Heon-seong's tombs. In their tombs, they wrote detailed accounts of the circumstances during their journey to the Tang, without any mention of regret for their misjudgment. Instead, they openly expressed their resentment towards Nam-geon and Nam-san, who betrayed them. They extensively justified and explained their own actions. Observing these brash tomb inscriptions may even provoke further anger towards their wrongdoings.

However, when I slightly shift my perspective, I can understand their sentiments to some extent. As high-ranking nobles, they enjoyed wealth and glory, but paradoxically, the inscriptions demonstrate that their lives in the Tang were not as comfortable as one might think. Moreover, the fact that they documented these detailed accounts about long-past events indicates that they could have carried the burden of their own mistakes until death.

7.
A Man Who Read the Tea Leaves and Left Goguryeo: Go Jog-yu

Among those who left for the Tang before the collapse of Goguryeo was Go Jog-yu (高足酉), who rose to a position as a Tang official next to that of Yeon Gaesomun's descendants. However, his existence would never have been known had it not been for the discovery of his epitaph. Go's tombstone was discovered in the north-western part of a village called Louzigou in Luoyang, Henan-sheng, China. The stone, which measures 58.5 centimeters in width and height, bears an epitaph consisting of 33 lines with 34 Chinese characters per line.

Records of Go Jog-yu are nowhere to be found in Chinese or Korean history books. However, after he moved to the Tang, he was appointed as Mingwei jiangjun (明威將軍)[101] and Shou youweiwei

101 'jiangjun (將軍)' means 'General' in Chinese.

zhenhuafu zhechongduwei reng zhangshang (守右威衛眞化府折冲都尉仍長上), and then as Shou zuoweiwei xiaoyifu zhexingduwe (守左威衛孝義府折衝都尉) in 668. The following year he was promoted to Yunhui jiangjun (雲麾將軍) and Xing zuowuwei yiweufu zhonglangjiang (行左武衛翊衛府中郎將). In 679 he became Youlingjun weijiangjun (右領軍衛將軍), and in 680 he received the title of Shangzhuguo (上柱國). In 689 Go became Youyuqianwei dajiangjun (右玉鈴衛大將軍), and the following year he became Zhenjun dajiangjun (鎭軍大將軍) and Zuobaotaowei dajiangjun (左豹韜衛大將軍). In 695 he was appointed Chief of Goryeo fanzhen (蕃長) and Yuyangjun kaiguogong (漁陽郡開國公). Instead of the descendants of King Bojang or Yeon Gaesomun, a man who was never mentioned in any historical records became Chief Envoy of Goguryeo, the representative position of the Goguryeo immigrants.

While the epitaph lists various positions Go Jog-yu held in the Tang Dynasty, it says nothing about his ancestry. It says that "he came from a wealthy family", but does not list the positions he held during their time in Goguryeo. Some scholars believe that he and his ancestors either came from a side branch of the royal family, or that the author of the epitaph did not know enough about his family background to include it in the description. The phrase "wealthy family" has led some scholars to believe that he was the son of a wealthy landowner. Unfortunately, the epitaph does not leave much room for conjecture. It records the activities in which this man from Pyongyang was involved as a Tang official, suggesting that he was a nobleman in Goguryeo, but not of such high rank as Cheon Heon-seong. This leads to the conclusion that Go Jog-yu had a successful career in the Tang because he earned it through his own efforts, rather than because of his former status or family background in Goguryeo.

According to his epitaph, Go Jog-yu was a man of great foresight. Sensing that Goguryeo was coming to an end, he moved his entire family to Tang territory when he was over 40 years old. Even if he had seen the signs that his homeland was on the verge of collapse, it would not have been easy for him at that age to take his whole family to the land of Goguryeo's enemy. He must have thought long and hard before making his decision. After emigrating to the Tang, he strove to rise through the ranks. When the Axis of Heaven was established, at the age of 70, he was treated as a representative of the Goguryeo immigrants. His name may have made it onto the elaborate monument created by top Tang artists to extol the virtues of Empress Wu. This must have been a hard-earned honor, earned through endless effort and heroism, risking his own fate and that of his entire family.

But death came at the height of his career. As Provincial Military Governor,[102] Go Jog-yu set out to conquer the Manzu (蠻族) and died of illness on his triumphant return to Jingzhou (荊州), near Xiangzhou

102 經略大使

(襄州) in Hebei-sheng, China. This suggests that despite his high status in the Tang, his life as a Goguryeo immigrant was not easy. He had to go to the battlefield at the age of 70. In fact, the average life expectancy of Goguryeo immigrants was not very long. Many were either executed on false charges, like Cheon Heon-seong, or died on the battlefields. Cheon Nam-sang lived to the age of 63, but Cheon Nam-saeng died at 46, Cheon Heon-seong at 42, Go Ja at 33, and Go Hyeon at 49. Cheon Bi died at the age of 22. Of course, only a handful of Goguryeo immigrants found their way into the historical record, so their cases are hardly sufficient to represent Goguryeo immigrants as a whole. Nevertheless, it is true that in most of the cases recorded, these people died in their 40s and 50s. Some of them who had made remarkable achievements still met tragic ends, including Cheon Heon-seong, Go Seon-ji (高仙芝), and Wang Mo-jung (王毛仲).

Go Jog-yu seems to have been a rare exception. Good military skills and luck may have helped him reach the age of 70, but judging by the way he named his son Jesin (帝臣), which literally means "the emperor's subject," political savvy may also have contributed to his longevity. Both the politically-savvy Go Jog-yu and the militarily-savvy Cheon Heon-seong must have had to work hard to survive in a foreign land. Whether they liked it or not, their Goguryeo background must have been a burden for them in their day. The same may be true of today's Koreans who live abroad or have changed their nationality. Wherever they are and whatever their nationality, the fact that they were born Korean will never be erased from their minds or their appearance.

8.
Men of Mohe or Goguryeo?: Yi Ta-in and Dae Jo-yeong

A Top Local Official of Chaekju, Yi Ta-in

In January 1989, the tomb of Yi Ta-in (李他仁) was discovered in a grave at the construction site of a cotton factory in northwest of Baqiao District (灞橋區), not far from present-day Xi'an in Shaanxi-sheng, China. When the tomb was built, Xi'an was called Chang'an and was the capital of the Tang Dynasty. Baqiao was the last bridge that people crossed on their way to the western regions. Because many people said goodbye to their lovers, husbands, or family members at the bridge, it has often been mentioned in poetry since the days of the Tang dynasty. It was also on the outskirts of Chang'an that many kings and nobles of the other ethnic groups subjugated by the Tang were buried.

King Bojang must have been buried nearby, apparently next to Illig Qaghan of the Eastern Turk Khaganate. After the fall of their kingdoms, King Bojang and Illig Qaghan stood side by side, like trophies, behind the Emperor at the great events of the Tang royal court, adding to His Majesty's dignity. When they died, the two were buried close together.

Yi Ta-in's epitaph states that he was a Liaodong person from Chaekju (柵州), and also mentions names such as Jumong, Goguryeo, Mohe, Yeong Gong (英公) and Yi Jeok (李勣). According to his epitaph, Yi Ta-in died in Tang in 675 at the age of 67, and was buried in his tomb on the 16th of second month, 677. Counting backwards, this means that he was born in Goguryeo in 609 and was 59 years old when the kingdom fell.

Yi Ta-in's grandfather Bok-chu (福鄒) held the rank of Daehyeong (大兄), while his father Maeng-jin (孟眞) served as Daesang (大相). In Goguryeo, Daehyeong was a rank 7 and Daesang, also known as Taedaesaja (太大使者), an upper rank 4. These details suggest that Yi Ta-in was born into a family of high-ranking officials. His epitaph also boasts that "all his family members brought glory to the East and made honorable contributions to Byeonhan, becoming pillars of the kingdom blessed with abundant wealth and honor."

Yi Ta-in was the Head of Protectorate (Dudu) and Military Commander of Chaekju.[103] Dudu was a Chinese public official equivalent

103 柵州 都督兼總兵馬

to Yoksal, a high-ranking local official in late Goguryeo. Since the reign of King Taejo (r. 53–146), Chaekju had been a central area in northeastern Goguryeo. It was mentioned under a different name in the *History of the Three Kingdoms*, which called it Chaekseong, and scholars believe that it was present-day Hunchun (琿春), China. The area had previously been part of northern Okjeo and was the first place Goguryeo invaded after establishing the kingdom along the Aprok River.

According to the *History of the Three Kingdoms*, Dongmyeong the Holy King, or Jumong of Goguryeo, sent Bu Wi-yeom (扶尉猒) to conquer northern Okjeo and turned the land into a fortified city in the eleventh month of 28 BCE. However, scholars question whether such developments actually took place during Jumong's reign. Southern Okjeo, centered on Hamheung, was later conquered during the reign of Taejo, the sixth king of Goguryeo. For this reason, some scholars have suggested that although Goguryeo's conquest of northern Okjeo took place after Jumong's time, it may simply have been added to the description for the sake of record. However, given the specific mention of Bu Wi-yeom's name and the fact that the area is related to eastern Buyeo, archaeological sources must be re-examined to determine exactly when Goguryeo conquered northern Okjeo.

In any case, Goguryeo gained control of northern and southern Okjeo early on and received regular tribute from them, such as fish, salt and beautiful women, until the middle of the third century.

Goguryeo briefly lost Okjeo in 245 when Guanqiu Jian ordered Wang Qi, governor of the Xuantu Commandery, to attack Okjeo, but soon regained control of it. Beginning from the fourth century, Goguryeo officials were sent to Okjeo to govern it directly. Todays' Hunchun and the surrounding area near the Tumen River came under the jurisdiction of Chaekju and served as the northeastern center of Goguryeo until the collapse of the kingdom.

From the sixth century onward, local governments in Goguryeo were divided into three tiers: daeseong, jeseong and seong. A yoksal was sent to oversee the top tier, the daeseong, while a cheoryeogeunji was sent to the middle tier, the jeseong, and a garadal and rucho to the bottom tier, the seong. Yoksal, as noted above, was a Goguryeo government post equivalent to the Dudu (都督) in China. Because the title "yoksal" is a Korean word without Chinese characters, Yi Ta-in-'s epitaph must have stated that he had served as Dudu of Chaekju, as the Tang people were unlikely to recognize it.

In those days, local officials exercised all administrative, judicial and military authority, so the highest ranking official in a given area could wield great power. When Yeon Gaesomun staged his coup, there was nothing he could do when the lord of Ansi Castle refused to side with him. This incident gives an idea of the power and authority wielded by top local officials at the time. From his office in Chaekseong, the Dudu of Chaekju oversaw all the areas along the Tuman River. The region was populated by people from northern

Okjeo and Buyeo, as well as the Maek and Yemaek tribes, who had helped found Goguryeo. The Goguryeo court had also strategically placed Han Chinese migrants and the Baishan Mohe in the region. They were all ruled by Yi Ta-in, who was in charge of 12 Goguryeo prefectures and 37 Mohe groups.

At the Forefront of the Attack on Pyongyang Castle

Yi Ta-in came from a family of high government officials. He enjoyed a good layer of wealth and great honor from his glorious achievements for the country. However, he surrendered to the Tang General Li Ji (李勣, 594–669), who was the commander-in-chief of the Tang forces attacking Goguryeo, just before the kingdom collapsed. However, the circumstances of Yi Ta-in's surrender remain unknown. He may have surrendered after a battle with the Tang forces, or, like Go Jog-yu, he may have fled the moment he sensed that Goguryeo's fall was imminent. Yi Ta-in's epitaph says only that "he realized that Goguryeo would collapse and knew whom to turn to after seeing a star fall into the Liang River (梁水)." Learning from the lesson of the Gongsun Clan (公孫氏) which had fallen to the Cao-Wei (曹魏, 220–265) forces in less than 100 days, he hurriedly led his troops to Li Ji's camp and surrendered. After Yi Ta-in's surrender, Li Ji had sent him and his men to the front of the invasion war against Goguryeo. Yi Ta-in led a large army to crush the Goguryeo Generals who had resisted so far, and succeeded in opening the door to Seok Fortress,[104] which had remained closed in defense against nine attacks. Yi Ta-in also led the Tang forces in capturing of Pyongyang Castle before following Li Ji back to the Tang. For his contributions to the conquest of Goguryeo, Ta-in was appointed to the position of a junior military official of rank 3, Yourongwei jiangjun.[105]

According to Yi Ta-in's epitaph, a movement to revive Goguryeo broke out in the former territory of Buyeo after he moved to the Tang interior. On the orders of the Tang court, Yi Ta-in went there to suppress the movement and eliminate its leader. Scholars believe that this incident took place between 670 and 671, preceding a similar attempt by King Bojang in 677. Upon his return to Liaodong, King Bojang had attempted to revive Goguryeo by joining forces with the Sumo Mohe (粟末靺鞨), but this attempt was discovered in advance and resulted in King Bojang's exile to Gongju.

The discovery of Yi Ta-in's tomb has helped to reveal details not recorded in other historical sources. While historical sources contain descriptions of the battles between Goguryeo and the Tang around the Liao River, the Aprok River, and Pyongyang Castle, they say nothing about the circumstances near the north-eastern border of Goguryeo. Yi Ta-in's epitaph indicates that the highest local official

---

104 石城

105 右戎衛將軍

in the area led his troops and voluntarily surrendered to the Tang, which explains how the Tang was able to take this area without lifting a finger and advance on Pyongyang Castle without having to worry about being attacked from that direction. It was previously known that there were revival movements of Goguryeo in Liaodong where the PGPE[106] was located, as well as in Hwanghae-do where Geom Mojam took the lead. However, through the epitaph of Yi Ta-in, it has become known that a revival movement also took place in the ancient Buyeo region. The epitaph also mentions that Yang Xuanji (陽玄基) killed Go Jeong-mun (高定問), the head of Chaekju, for rebelling. After Yi Ta-in's surrender and the collapse of Goguryeo, the Tang had made Chaekju a vassal province and appointed Go Jeong-mun as head of the Goguryeo migrants in the area to minimize their resistance. Yang Xuanji was appointed as the Tang official to keep an eye on Go Jeong-mun, who eventually staged a revolt. This suggests that when the Tang began to control Goguryeo as a vassal state in the early 670s, movements to revive Goguryeo were active in many places. The epitaph of one individual thus fills a gap in the picture of the overall situation at that time that other historical records have failed to fill.

For suppressing the movement to revive Goguryeo in the former Buyeo area, the Tang emperor bestowed on Yi Ta-in the title, General

---

106 安東都護府, Protectorate-General to Pacify the East

of the Right Wing[107] of the Central Administration.[108] The General of the Right Wing was the same rank as Yourongwei jiangjun that was given to Yi Ta-in just after his first appearance at the Tang imperial court. For this reason, some suggest that his contributions to the suppression of the Goguryeo revivalist movements were either minimal or not properly recognized by the Tang court. Others suggest that the bestowal of this title signified a promotion from a position outside the central administration to a role within it.

In any case, Yi Ta-in had become a Tang General who took the lead in destroying his homeland of Goguryeo and suppressing movements to revive it. Seven years after the Tang took Pyongyang Castle, Yi Ta-in died of illness at his home in Chang'an in 675, aged 67. Having spent 60 years of his life as a Goguryeo man and only seven years as a Tang subject, he was buried far from Goguryeo in Xi'an.

Dae Jo-yeong, from Yingzhou to Mount Dongmo

Dae Jo-yeong was posthumously named King Go (高王), the first ruler of Balhae between 698 and 719. After the fall of Goguryeo, Dae Jo-yeong resided in Yingzhou (營州) until two Khitan men, Li Jinzhong (李盡式) and Sun Wanrong (孫萬榮), staged a revolt in 696. In

107 右領軍將軍

108 同正員

the ensuing chaos, Dae Jo-yeong fled east with his father, Geolgeol Jungsang (乞乞仲象), a Mohe chieftain called Qisi Biyu (乞四比羽), and Goguryeo refugees willing to follow them. However, a recent study has suggested that they participated in the Khitan uprising rather than using it as an opportunity to flee Yingzhou.

When Goguryeo fell, the Tang selected 38,200 wealthy and powerful Goguryeo families and forced them to relocate to their territory. Goguryeo's former land was turned into a vassal prefecture, and the rest of the Goguryeo people were ruled by PGPE. Yingzhou, now Chaoyang (朝阳) in China's Liaoning-sheng, was a central area of the Liaoxi region where the Tang established a vassal prefecture populated by other ethnic groups. The influence of foreign customs was strong, as various ethnic groups such as the Goguryeo people, the Mohe, the Khitans, the Xianbei, and the Xi (奚族) lived there alongside the Han Chinese. Due to the area's proximity to a Khitan community, there were many Khitans in the area, as well as a considerable number of immigrants from Goguryeo. Some had been forced to leave their hometowns due to the Goguryeo-Tang war and had wandered into the area. Some had intended to move further into Tang territory as part of the collective relocation policy, but decided to stay in the area. Even after a group of Dae Jo-yeong fled and founded Balhae, there were a number of Goguryeo people who remained in Yingzhou. Perhaps the best known of these was Yi Jeong-gi, who later moved to Shandong-sheng.

With regard to the founding of Balhae, the accounts of the relationships between the leading figures differ slightly depending on the historical source. The *Old Book of Tang*[109] says that Dae Jo-yeong and Qisi Biyu were the ones who led the Goguryeo people out of Yingzhou. However, the *Institutions of the Five Dynasties Period*[110] and the *New Book of Tang* say that Dae Jo-yeong's father, Geolgeol Jungsang, and Qisi Biyu led the people at first, and that Dae Jo-yeong took over after his father died. Under Empress Wu's rule, the Tang's first priority was to pacify the Khitans, so there were no resources left to stop the exodus of Goguryeo immigrants. Instead, as a conciliatory measure, the Tang gave titles to Goguryeo leaders to keep them under its control. It offered Dae Jo-yeong the title of Zhenguogong (震國公)[111] and Qisi Biyu the title of Xuguogong (許國公),[112] but Qisi Biyu refused to accept his.

The Tang finally succeeded in suppressing the Khitan revolt by hiring the Turk Mo Chuo (默啜). In 698, the Tang sent troops to hunt down the Goguryeo migrants. The person who led these troops was Li Kaigu (李楷固), a Khitan General who had surrendered to the Tang. Under Li's command, the Tang forces defeated the Goguryeo people led by Qisi Biyu, who died in battle. Dae Jo-yeong had already taken

---

109 *Jiu Tangshu* (『舊唐書』)

110 *Wudai Huiyao* (『五代會要』)

111 It can be translated as "Duke of the Powerful Territory."

112 It can be translated as "Duke of Xu Country."

over his father's leadership role. After Qisi Biyu's death, he headed east rallying the remaining people, many of whom were of Mohe descent and had no idea where to go and headed east. His men fought for their lives in a great battle with the Tang forces at Mount Tianmen (天門嶺) near Changlingzi (長嶺子), a watershed that divides the Hun River (渾河) and the Huifa River (輝發河). After a fierce battle, they finally defeated their enemy. However, the risk of being pursued by more Tang troops left them no time to enjoy their victory, and Dae Jo-yeong urged them to continue eastward. They arrived at Mt. Dongmo,[113] at the site of the present-day city of Dunhua in Jilin-sheng, and it was there that Dae Jo-yeong founded the nation of Jin (震) that same year 698, and began using their own era name of Cheontong (天統).

Mt. Dongmo was far from the center of the Tang Empire, and there were no other major powers nearby, making it an appropriate place for a group of migrants like Dae Jo-yeong to found a new country. Eastern Manchuria had come under Tang rule after the collapse of Goguryeo, but the Tang had failed to gain a firm grip on the region due to the resistance of the Goguryeo people there. Under these circumstances, the group led by Dae Jo-yeong escaped from Yingzhou and established a state. The Goguryeo migrants, who had been scattered throughout the country, immediately flocked to Mt. Dongmo. Some of them were from the Maek and Yemaek tribes who

113 東牟山

had helped to found Goguryeo, and many of them were Mohe. A group of Baishan Mohe[114] had lived in this region as Goguryeo citizens, and the region itself was near a Sumo Mohe[115] community. In other words, the region had been part of Goguryeo for so long that its inhabitants had little reason to reject Dae Jo-yeong and the people he brought with him. Seeing no need to start a war to establish control over somewhere as distant as Mt. Dongmo, the Tang did not send any more troops after them. When Dae Jo-yeong officially sent an envoy, the Tang hesitantly received him and appointed Dae Jo-yeong as the King of Balhae.[116] Around this time, the state began to use the name Balhae. Balhae declared itself the successor to Buyeo and Goguryeo and even made a formal declaration to Japan. Thus, thirty years after the fall of Goguryeo, its successor emerged from its former region on the northeastern border. Dae Jo-yeong died in 719, and his son Dae Muye (大武藝) ascended the throne as the second king of Balhae, now known as King Mu.

---

114 白山靺鞨

115 粟末靺鞨

116 渤海郡王

Yi Ta-in and Dae Jo-yeong: Were They of Goguryeo or Mohe Descent?

Yi Ta-in and Dae Jo-yeong were on completely opposite sides in terms of active regions, experiences, and burial places. One thing they have in common, however, is that they have been the subject of ongoing debate as to whether they were of Goguryeo or Mohe descent.

Yi Ta-in's epitaph does not deify the founder of Goguryeo, Jumong, and disrespectfully refers to the Goguryeo kings as "sons of Jumong's concubines." As Dudu of Chaekju, Yi Ta-in ruled over 12 Goguryeo prefectures and 37 Mohe groups. However, none of the Goguryeo people who surrendered to the Tang originally had Yi as their family name. In fact, Yi was a surname that the Tang sometimes gave to non-Han Chinese tribal leaders. For these reasons, there has been much speculation about Yi Ta-in's ethnicity. Some argue that he was a Sumo Mohe or a Mohe who had settled in Chaekseong, and some argue that he was a Goguryeo person born into a family that had produced generations of high-ranking government officials. Others argue that it is impossible to tell from his epitaph alone whether he was a pure Goguryeo person or a Goguryeo person of Mohe descent.

As for Dae Jo-yeong, opinions have been divided since the time when the *Old Book of Tang* and the *New Book of Tang* were compiled. The *Old Book of Tang* says that Qisi Biyu was a Mohe, but it doesn't say anything about Dae Jo-yeong. The *New Book of Tang* and the *Wudai Huiyao*, on the other hand, say that Dae Jo-yeong came from a branch of Goryeo people.

The terms "Goguryeo people" and "Mohe" are used when discussing the families of Yi Ta-in and Dae Jo-yeong, or the groups led by Dae Jo-yeong and Qisi Biyu, because history books make a distinction between Goguryeo and Mohe. However, it may be necessary to consider the validity of such terms.

Chaekju, once ruled by Yi Ta-in, was home to many Baishan Mohe in the seventh century. The Sumo Mohe, which some associate with Dae Jo-yeong, were scattered throughout Buyeo. Chaekseong, in the center of Chaekju, had long been part of Goguryeo territory and had remained stable until the kingdom's collapse. Goguryeo had also begun to make inroads into Buyeo in the late third century, and by the fourth century it was sending officials to directly govern its lands there.

With the exception of the Heishu Mohe, the rest of the seven Mohe tribes were all under Goguryeo control. Goguryeo may not have ruled the Boduo Mohe, Haoshi Mohe, Anchegu Mohe, and Funie Mohe directly, but historical records show that these tribes scattered after the collapse of Goguryeo, and their whereabouts became a mystery. This suggests that they were indirectly ruled or influenced by Goguryeo. The Baishan Mohe and Sumo Mohe, on the other hand, had been incorporated into Goguryeo earlier than the other Mohe tribes, and their natural environment was not so different from that of

Goguryeo, which explains why they lived as Goguryeo people from the early days.

Goguryeo was a multiethnic state formed by the union of the Maek people of the middle Aprok River basin and the Ye people of Buyeo. After these regions were incorporated into Goguryeo, the state continued to expand, bringing a variety of other tribes into its realm. Goguryeo conquered all of Liaodong, extending north to what is now the Russian Far East and south to below the Han River. Goguryeo's domain was thus inhabited by various groups of people, including the Xianbei, Khitans, Mohe, Han Koreans (韓族), and Han Chinese (漢族), all of whom considered themselves Goguryeo people. Of course, the Ye, Maek, and Yemaek may have played a central role in the establishment of Goguryeo, but other ethnic groups that joined them later were also governed by Goguryeo laws, paid taxes to the Goguryeo government, and fought to protect Goguryeo and their families whenever they were attacked by invading Yan or Tang forces. They were all Goguryeo people.

However, there were still differences among the ethnic groups. Some led their own lifestyles that were different from those of Goguryeo, and they were allowed to maintain their unique lifestyles under Goguryeo rule. For example, the Mohe, unlike other Goguryeo people, lived in tribal communities in an environment where it was difficult for them to pay taxes in grain. The Goguryeo government therefore allowed them to pay less in taxes in exchange for providing more military services, and collected taxes from them on a group rather than individual basis. According to one historical source, a unit of Mohe troops that fought for Goguryeo in a war against the Tang served as a special unit. However, descriptions in the *Old Book of Tang* and *New Book of Tang* make a distinction between the Mohe and the Goguryeo people, which has been repeated in other publications and continues to cause unnecessary confusion about the identity of the Mohe.

How were the Mohe who lived in Goguryeo regarded by the other Goguryeo people and governed by the Goguryeo government? The answer can be found in Yi Ta-in's epitaph, which states that Ta-in governed 12 Goguryeo prefectures and 37 Mohe groups. This description indicates that the Goguryeo people and the Mohe had the same nationality and were equally recognized as residents of Chaekju. However, the Mohe had a different way of life, so the administrative units for them needed to be different. Therefore, they were divided into groups rather than prefectures. Anyone who did not belong to a Mohe group would have been classified as a member of one of the 12 prefectures. However, they all believed that they were residents of Chaekju and people of Goguryeo.

Some say that Korea has been a multicultural society since the days of Dangun,[117] its mythical ancestor. The reason for this is that

---

117 檀君

Dangun was born from the marriage of Hwanung, who descended from heaven, and Ungnyeo, a bear who turned into a woman with Hwanung's help. However, many Koreans still believe that Korea was originally a mono-ethnic nation, even though there is no factual, scientific evidence to support this belief. Similar irrational thinking is sometimes applied to the Mohe who lived as members of Goguryeo society. They regard the Mohe as non-Koreans, while Balhae is still a part of Korean history because it succeeded Goguryeo. Balhae was founded by a large number of Mohe together with a few Goguryeo people. It is true that Balhae claimed to be the successor of Goguryeo. Even though Dae Jo-yeong and Yi Ta-in may have been of Yemaek or Mohe descent, the fact that they were both Goguryeo people will never change. Therefore, it is useless to question whether the Mohe really belonged to the Goguryeo people or to accept the distinction drawn between the Mohe and the Goguryeo people in Chinese historical records.

9.
Goguryeo as Roots or Fetters?: Go Seon-ji and Yi Jeong-gi

Go Seon-ji's Ambition

Go Seon-ji (高仙芝, Ch. Gao Xianzhi) was born in China to a Goguryeo immigrant family. His father, Go Sa-gye (高舍鷄), was originally stationed in the Hexi Army (河西軍) but was later transferred to Anxi, and Go Seon-ji followed him there. Go Sa-gye accumulated military achievements, serving as the Commander of Four Garrisons and General of Various Guards.

Thanks to his father, Go Seon-ji became a garrison commander, at an early age and soon rose to the same rank as his father. He is said to have been a graceful, handsome man with a brave and determined character who was highly skilled in horseback riding and archery. Although his performance remained ordinary while serving under the military governors,[118] Tian Renwan (田仁琬) and Gai Jiayun (蓋嘉運), he distinguished himself on several occasions after being recommended by Fumeng Lingcha (夫蒙靈察). He was promoted to Yanqi (焉耆) Regional Commander,[119] and in the late Kaiyuan era (開元, 713–741), he rose to the positions of the Vice Protector-General to Pacify the West[120] and the Military Commander of Four Garrisons[121] after conquering Daxibu (達奚部) west of the Tianshan Mountains with two thousand troops.

In 747, Go Seon-ji made a name for himself when he successfully led an expedition against Lesser Bolü (小勃律國).[122] At the time, the Tang was expanding its power as it competed with the Islamic caliphate in the area around the Pamir Plateau, and the states caught between them were forced to choose sides for their own preservation. The rather powerful Tubo (吐蕃, Tibet) chose to ally with the Islamic caliphate and attempted to march eastward to keep the Tang at bay. This prompted Tang Emperor Xuanzong (r. 712–756)[123] to appoint Go Seon-ji as the Field Commanding General[124] and order him to conquer the Tibetans.

118 節度使

119 焉耆鎮守使

120 安西副都護

121 四鎭都知兵馬使

122 小勃律國, It was a city state around modern Gilgit, Pakistan.

123 唐 玄宗

124 行營節度使

Go Seon-ji led ten thousand troops through Shighnan (五識匿國) and across the Pamir Plateau to destroy the Tibetan military base called Kansir Fort. During the battle, the Tang forces killed five thousand of their enemies and captured one thousand. They also captured a thousand horses and a large cache of weapons and provisions. Go Seon-ji's army then continued its advance and climbed the Darkot Pass in the Hindu Kush Mountains to occupy the capital of Lesser Bolü (阿弩越城). It then cut the bridge leading to Tubo and the Islamic lands. As a result of his success in obtaining the surrender of 72 states, including the Dashi (大食國, Arabs),[125] Go Seon-ji rose to the position of Acting Deputy Chief of Protocol,[126] and in 749 he was appointed as the Special Advisor and General of the Capital Security.[127]

In 750 (the 9th year of Tianbao era of Tang emperor Xuanzong), Go Seon-ji embarked on his second western campaign. This was because Shiguo (石國 modern Tashkent), located along the Syr Darya River west of the Pamir Mountains, had surrendered to the Islamic caliphate. The Tang felt compelled to punish Shiguo lest this betrayal encourages other forces under their control to surrender. Go Seon-ji set out with an army of 100,000 men. Everyone thought it impossible to lead an army over the Tianshan Mountains, but Go Seon-ji defied the odds and succeeded. He reached Shiguo, took the castle by siege, and

---

125 大食國

126 鴻臚卿攝御史中丞

127 特進兼左金吾大將軍同正員

brought the king and princess back to Chang'an as prisoners. This impressed the Tang central government enough to grant him the title of Kaifu yitong sansi.[128] In addition to a higher status and reputation, he also came to own two lavish houses in Chang'an. Historical records say that Go Seon-ji was greedy and looted large amounts of treasure, horses, and weapons in the process of conquering Shiguo. However, in those days, looting was generally the greatest incentive for going to war, so it is hard to say that Go Seon-ji was unique in his greed for booty. Perhaps some envied the wealth and prestige he had gained by successfully leading two western campaigns.

Go Seon-ji's luck began to run out on his third western campaign. During the previous campaign, his Tang forces had sacked Shiguo and brought its king back to Chang'an, where he was beheaded. This had aroused animosity against the Tang in the western regions and led to an armed alliance around the Islamic caliphate. In 751 (the 10th year of Tianbao era of the Tang emperor Xuanzong), Go Seon-ji set out with 70,000 troops to attack this allied arm forces. However, the Tang forces were defeated in a great battle at Talas, north of the Pamir Mountains, when their supposed allies, the Karluk Turks, betrayed them and attacked them from behind. This was the world-famous Battle of Talas. Despite this defeat, Emperor Xuanzong must still have had confidence in Go Seon-ji, because he appointed

128 開府儀同三司, A title bestowed in recognition of the meritorious contributions made through government service.

him Hexi military governor[129] and Grand General of the Imperial Guards.[130] In 755, Go Seon-ji was given the title of Duke of Mirun.[131]

In the eleventh month of the same year, An Lushan (安祿山, 703–757) instigated a rebellion in Fanyang (范陽, today's Beijing). When his rebel forces marched on Chang'an, the Tang court appointed Go Seon-ji the Deputy Commander for Counterinsurgency[132] and ordered him to subdue them. The rebels wanted to seize Tongguan (潼關, Tong Pass), a key point on the way to Chang'an, and overpowered Feng Changqing (封常清), a General close to Go Seon-ji and a military governor who had been assigned to guard Tongguan. Go Seon-ji had been ordered to stay in Shanzhou (陝州) at that time, but he thought it was more important to defend Tongguan, so he set out with his men without waiting for permission from his superior. Before leaving, however, he opened the doors of the Taiyuan granary[133] and distributed all the grain and silk in the granary to his men to prevent the goods from falling into the hands of the rebels.

Bian Lingcheng (邊令誠), a eunuch who harbored a grudge against Go Seon-ji, saw this as an opportunity to frame him. Bian informed Emperor Xuanzong that Go Seon-ji had retreated in fear and

---

129 河西節度使

130 右羽林軍大將軍

131 密雲郡公

132 討賊副元帥

133 太原倉

was embezzling supplies from the government storehouse. Enraged by the news, the emperor ordered Go Seon-ji to be beheaded immediately. Go Seon-ji thus met his death at the front, after the execution of Feng Changqing, with whom he had shared joys and sorrows for many years, at the hands of assassins brought in by Bian Lingcheng. When he was attacked, Go Seon-ji was surrounded by men he had personally chosen to serve at his side. Just before he died, he said to them, "I led you here to defend Tongguan, so I suppose I can be blamed for retreating. But it is a slander to say that I have embezzled something. If I really did embezzle, then you should not hesitate to say so. But if I have not, then say that I have been wronged. Then all the men shouted, "He has been wronged," and the sound was so loud that the ground shook under their feet.

Go Seon-ji was a great Tang General of Goguryeo descent who rose to high positions due to his outstanding achievements, even making it into biographies included in history books. During his rise, however, he was often slandered and viewed with jealousy by those around him. Even Fumeng Lingcha, who first recognized Go Seon-ji's abilities and highly recommended him, hurled these humiliating words at Go Seon-ji: "Eat dog entrails, you Goguryeo scum! Eat dog shit!" when he learned that Go Seon-ji had failed to report a victory to him first.

As a descendant of a fallen kingdom, one can only imagine how much humiliation and discrimination Go Seon-ji had to endure in order to make something of himself in the Tang court, the very enemy that had overthrown Goguryeo. Perhaps the only way he could survive and gain wealth and prestige as a man from a ruined country was by actively participating in wars and demonstrating his military prowess.

Go Seon-ji became a famous figure in world history because he contributed to the cultural exchange along the Silk Road between East and West. It was neither intentional nor successful, but it was the Battle of Talas that led to the spread of Chinese papermaking technology to West Asia, making a significant contribution to the history of civilization. The British archaeologist Aurel Stein even commented that Go Seon-ji's ingenious strategies and tactics, as well as his ability as a military commander in the conquest of Tubo (Tibet), were greater than those of Hannibal or Napoleon. Thus, he became known as a hero in world history before he became known in Korean or Chinese history.

In this sense, Go Seon-ji's achievements tend to be magnified in discussions of Goguryeo. As impressive as they were, one cannot help but wonder why a man with such outstanding military skills did not attempt to restore Goguryeo. Of course, when he was active, many years had passed since the collapse of Goguryeo, and the Protectorate-General to Pacify the West where he was stationed was on the opposite side of the country from where Goguryeo had been. The Goguryeo people had been relocated far from their homeland to ensure that they would not attempt to revive Goguryeo. Therefore, even if there had been soldiers of Goguryeo descent, it would have been difficult to motivate them to unite for the purpose of restoring Goguryeo. The Goguryeo people scattered throughout the borderlands would already have been struggling to survive in barren places far from home. Therefore, it is reasonable that the son of a Goguryeo native who had served as a low-ranking official, Go Seon-ji, deserves a positive appraisal for striving to improve his military skills and acquire wealth and prestige on his own.

Yi Jeong-gi's Dream

The real name of Yi Jeong-gi (李正己, Ch. Li Zhengji) was Hoe-ok (懷玉). He was born in Pinglu (平盧), Yingzhou, a vassal prefecture established by the Tang to govern the Goguryeo people, the Khitans, and the Xianbei. Yi Hoe-ok became an assistant General[134] stationed at Pinglu Circuit. When the governor of Pinglu, Wang Xuanzhi (王玄志) died in 758, the Tang court intended to appoint his son as the military provincial governor of Pinglu. However, Yi Hoe-ok killed Wang Xuanzhi's son and recommended his own cousin Hou Xiyi (侯希逸) for the post. Hoe-ok was 26 years old at the time.

134 裨將

Pinglu was located near the base of An Lushan and Shi Siming (史思明), but it was opposed to An Lushan's stance. This left the military province in a difficult position, cut off from the Tang court and threatened by An Lushan's army to the west and the Xi to the north. After some deliberation, Hou Xiyi and Yi Hoe-ok led 20,000 troops from Pinglu to Dengzhou (登州) in Shandong and then joined the central government army in Qingzhou (青州). The Tang court appreciated their decision to march across the sea rather than join the rebels, and subsequently appointed Hou Xiyi as military governor of Pinglu ziqing.[135]

Unfortunately, Hou Xiyi then became absorbed in Buddhism, and instead of attending to administrative matters, he pushed ahead with the construction of a large temple. Dissatisfaction with Hou Xiyi grew, while Yi Hoe-ok's popularity continued to rise. Fearing that he would be replaced, Hou Xiyi dismissed Yi Hoe-ok. However, the public objected to his actions, insisting that Yi Hoe-ok had done nothing to deserve dismissal. The public demanded that Hou Xiyi be removed and that Yi Hoe-ok take his place.

The Tang court bestowed Yi Hoe-ok with the new name "Jeong-gi" and appointed him military provincial governor of Pinglu ziqing. He was to simultaneously serve other government posts.[136] Not long

---

135 平盧淄青節度使

136 Haiyun ya bohai xinluo liangfanshi (海運押渤海新羅兩蕃使), Jianxiao gongbushangshu (檢校工部尚書), Yushi dafu (御史大夫), and Qingzhou cishi (青州刺史).

after, Yi Jeong-gi was also to serve as Jianxiao shangshu youpuye (右僕射) and was given the title of Raoyang junwang (饒陽郡王). In the tenth month of 776, he became Jianxiao sikong (檢校司空) Tongzhongshu menxia pingzhangshi (同中書門下平章事). The reason the Tang court continued to promote Yi Jeong-gi was because they wanted to contain his growing influence. Yi Jeong-gi had been trusted to govern ten prefectures: Zizhou (淄州), Qingzhou (青州), Qizhou (齊州), Haizhou (海州), Dengzhou (登州), Laizhou (萊州), Yizhou (沂州), Mizhou (密州), Dezhou (德州), and Dizhou (棣州). Five more, Caozhou (曹州), Puzhou (濮州), Xuzhou (徐州), Yanzhou (兗州), and Yunzhou (鄆州), were later added to the list. His rank also continued to rise, to Taizitaibo (太子太保) and Situ (司徒). His power grew to a level that threatened not only the Tang court, but also the nearby military provinces known as "fanzhen (藩鎮)."

The Tang court therefore set out to check Yi Jeong-gi, who in turn stationed troops at Jiyin (濟陰) as a countermeasure. He also sent more troops to Xuzhou to occupy the areas along the Yangtze and Huai rivers and take over the Grand Canal. No longer able to use the canal to transport supplies to the capital, the Tang court was forced to find an alternative route. The growing tension between the court and Yi Jeong-gi was about to erupt into a clash. Unfortunately, just as Luoyang and Chang'an were within his reach, Yi Jeong-gi came to an abrupt end, dying at the age of 49 from an abscess on his back. Relieved, the Tang court awarded him the title of Taiwei (太尉) posthumously. Yi Jeong-gi's son, Yi Nap (李納), kept his father's death a secret for months, fearing that the news would upset the people. He then regrouped his forces, proclaimed the establishment of a kingdom called Qi (齊國), and named himself its king. Qi maintained its status as an independent state under the reigns of Yi Nap's sons, Yi Sago (李師古) and Yi Sado (李師道), until finally falling to a joint attack by the Tang and several fanzhens in the 2nd month of 819.

Yi Jeong-gi is known to have been an agile, strong, and brave man. During the Baoying era (r. 762) , when several armies came to Dingzhou (定州) to subdue Shi Chaoyi (史朝義), the Huihe army had a leader who was boorish and rude, and several military governors gave in to him. Yi Jeong-gi decided to clip his wings and challenged him to a wrestling match with the agreement that the winner would beat the loser. After winning, Yi Jeong-gi grabbed the Huihe leader by the neck and struck him on the back. He was so overpowered that he did not dare to do anything cruel after that. This episode from the historical records shows how strong Jeong-gi was. He is also described as a calm, confident man, which suggests the depth of his character.

Yi Jeong-gi's decisions to help Hou Xiyi become a military governor and to lead Pinglu's forces across the sea to Shandong are noteworthy. At that time, Balhae was occupying the former territory of Goguryeo. Yi Jeong-gi's biography in the *Old Book of Tang*, on the other hand, begins by stating that he was a Goguryeo person. This indicates that even though Goguryeo had collapsed many years before, Jeong-gi retained his ancestral identity so that everyone would know that he was a descendant of Goguryeo.

But why did he go to Shandong instead of Balhae, which claimed to be the successor of Goguryeo? Although many Goguryeo immigrants lived in the Pinglu area, not all of them were from Goguryeo, judging from the fact that Yi Jeong-gi's cousin Hou Xiyi was Chinese. Perhaps going to Balhae was not an option in the first place. However, it could not have been easy to plan a mass relocation to an area like Dengzhou where people had no ties. Considering how quickly Yi Jeong-gi gained control over 15 prefectures after becoming the military governor of Pinglu ziqing, it seems that he was not only exceptionally competent, but also had the support of the powerful people in Pinglu.

This is reminiscent of the Goguryeo people who were forcibly relocated to the interior of China. After capturing Pyongyang Castle, Tang forced 38,200 wealthy and powerful families to move to Shannan (山南), Jingxi (京西), and Qizhou, as well as the southern part of Jianghuai (江淮). This is how the transfer was described in the *Outstanding Models from the Cachet of Literature*:[137] "The Goguryeo prisoners were sent to the west of the desert. Since they were scattered throughout Qingzhou and Xuzhou, it was easier to keep an eye

137 『册府元龜』

on them and make them work hard to till the land." This suggests the likelihood that Jeong-gi and his followers were aware of the groups of Goguryeo immigrants at their destination, who would be an asset to them in expanding their influence in the area rapidly.

Another background that helped Yi Jeong-gi expand his influence was that he had enough financial resources. Before his appointment as Haiyun ya bohai xinluo liangfanshi,[138] Yi Jeong-gi had already overseen the Tang's trade with Balhae and Silla. Dengzhou was the closest point in China accessible by sea from both Liaodong and the Korean peninsula, so the coast was populated by many immigrants from Goguryeo, Baekje, and Silla. Yi Jeong-gi used these human and military resources to control maritime trade, amass wealth, and expand his influence. Once he took control of Dizhou (棣州), he was able to accumulate additional wealth by monopolizing the salt from the Dizhou salt ponds and Haduo (蛤朶) in Shandong. He also profited greatly by regulating the entry of cargo ships passing through the canal, thereby dominating the region's distribution network. Thanks to their economic and military prowess, Yi Jeong-gi and his descendants were able to maintain the quasi-independence of their state for nearly five decades.

This was the reason why the Tang court and numerous neighboring fanzhens could not allow the Qi kingdom to expand its influ-

138 海運押新羅渤海兩蕃使, A position responsible for managing all diplomatic affairs and exchanges with Silla and Balhae.

ence. So they joined forces to attack Qi. When the Qi forces led by Yi Sado were defeated by the allied forces, Jang Bogo of Silla was a member of the army that attacked them, the Wuning Army (武寧軍). Just as Goguryeo had fallen to Silla with the help of the Tang, a state founded by a descendant of Goguryeo again fell to a Silla native. As a young man, Jang Bogo had left Silla for the Tang and gained influence there, especially in the Silla community of Shandong. He went on to establish a naval and trading base called Cheonghaejin and became a dominant figure in maritime trade between Silla, the Tang, and Japan. In a sense, all of this was possible because of the economic base, political network, and military resources that Yi Jeong-gi and his family had previously established.

As it turns out, Yi Jeong-gi played an important role in Korean history, especially during the Unified Silla and Balhae periods, in international trade and politics involving the Yellow Sea. However, his activities are not as well-known as those of Go Seon-ji. One of the main reasons for this is probably that he left the areas along the Liao River for the central plains, making him a peripheral figure in both Korean and Chinese history.

As a non-Han Chinese of Goguryeo descent, Yi Jeong-gi became a military provincial leader powerful enough to be considered a threat to the Tang court. While some of his activities were related to Silla and Balhae, there is no indication in historical sources that he was vocal about his Goguryeo background. Perhaps sailing from Yingzhou to Dengzhou was in itself a clear statement that he intended to play an active role in the Jungwon (中原, Central China) as a Tang citizen. However, he never made it into mainstream politics, nor did he become a prominent figure in Chinese history. Korean historians have been slow to acknowledge his existence. He may be an attractive subject for some who want to glorify Goguryeo and Korean history, but he himself did not emphasize his Goguryeo background. Moreover, the status of Goguryeo immigrants in Korean history remains mostly unknown, which may explain why he has been neglected by most scholars. We also tend to focus on the current national historical perspective when studying historical figures like him. However, like Go Seon-ji, Yi Jeong-gi's identity as a descendant of Goguryeo migrants followed him throughout his life, whether he wanted it or not—and whether it was a fetter or not.

II

Goguryeo Women, the Hero Makers

1.
The Women Behind Jumong: Lady Yuhwa, Lady Ye, and Soseono

Yi Gyu-bo's Version of Lady Yuhwa

Lady Yuhwa plays a minor role in the founding myth of Goguryeo. In historical sources such as *History of the Three Kingdoms*, *Memoirs of the Three Kingdoms*, and Book of Wei, she is described as the daughter of Habaek, the wife of Haemosu, or the mother of Jumong. In the abridged versions of the myth that appear on the Tomb Stele of King Gwanggaeto and in Moduru's epitaph, her presence is omitted, and her son Jumong is referred to as the "grandson of Habaek." Lady Yuhwa's role remains limited in the descriptions of the *History of the Three Kingdoms*, which is known to contain various rewrites presenting Confucian views of traditional tales, and in the *Memoirs of the Three Kingdoms*, which is based primarily on the

History of the Three Kingdoms and other Chinese sources. Was she then nothing more than someone's daughter, wife, or mother? It may seem futile to seriously analyze a mythical figure. Myths are mixtures of historical facts and later elements that reflect the societies and times in which they were created or transmitted. Therefore, analyzing Lady Yuhwa can provide insight into Goguryeo and Goryeo societies in later period.

Among the founding myths of Goguryeo, the richest portrayal of what Lady Yuhwa accomplished is found in *Saga of King Dongmyeong*[1], included in the *Collected Works of Minister Yi of the Eastern State*,[2] written by Yi Gyu-bo (1168–1241). The *Saga of King Dongmyeong* is an epic saga that Yi Gyu-bo was inspired to write after coming across the founding myth of Goguryeo in the *Old History of the Three Kingdoms*,[3] which was published before the *History of the Three Kingdoms*. When Yi Gyu-bo first heard about the strange, extraordinary episodes involving King Dongmyeong, he laughed and said, "Old Master Zhongni (仲尼, Confucius) did not talk about extraordinary things, feats of strength, disturbances, or spiritual beings. The story of King Dongmyeong is so strange and far-fetched that it is not worth discussing."

Then, in the fourth month of 1193 (the 24th year of Goryeo Myung-

1 「東明王」

2 『東國李相國集』

3 『舊三國史』

jong[4]), he managed to get a copy of *Old Version of History of the Three Kingdoms* and read the *Annals of King Dongmyeong*.[5] The episodes in the biography turned out to be even more marvelous than what he had heard before. Since the contents were mythical, he said, "At first I could only regard them as fantasy or illusion, but after going through the episodes three more times and looking into their origins, I realized that they were sacred rather than illusory and divine rather than fantasy." As a result, he changed his thought on the story of King Dongmyeong, believing that it could not be a fabrication because it was written as part of a nation's history and must be based on facts.

Yi Gyu-bo explained his purpose in writing *Saga of King Dongmyeong* as follows: "The miraculous events surrounding King Dongmyeong were not recounted to dazzle people, but to convey the incredible foundation of a nation. What would posterity think if such episodes were omitted from the history of the nation? Therefore, this epic was written to leave a record and let the whole world know that our country was originally a land of holy people."

Nowadays, we make our children read western epics like The Iliad and The Odyssey from elementary school on, but we tend to pay less attention to the *Saga of King Dongmyeong*, a Korean epic that is ancient, magnificent, and impressive and surpasses them.

Yi Gyu-bo's *Saga of King Dongmyeong* unfolds like a fanta-

4 高麗 明宗

5 「東明王本紀」

sy movie in which Haemosu comes down from heaven and meets Lady Yuhwa. Later, the abandoned and exiled Lady Yuhwa is put in the hands of King Geumwa of Buyeo, where she becomes pregnant by the sunlight that enters her room. Jumong is born as an egg and suffers persecution until he flees to the south and establishes Goguryeo. The recent movie *Along with the Gods*[6] has shown that Korean fantasies with the help of computer graphic techniques have great potential for entertainment. Perhaps Jumong's founding of Goguryeo and Yi Gyu-bo's epic *Saga of King Dongmyeong* can be made into a movie one day.

While Jumong is the most prominent protagonist, the *Saga of King Dongmyeong* also devotes a fair amount of attention to Lady Yuhwa, unlike other historical sources that keep descriptions of her deeds to a minimum. The scenes in which she meets and falls in love with Haemosu are fascinating and set the epic apart from other versions of Goguryeo's founding myth. Although the story is set more than two thousand years ago, what happens to Lady Yuhwa involves issues of love, marriage, and childbirth that are surprisingly similar to those faced by people today. After being abandoned by Haemosu, Lady Yuhwa was rebuked by her father and sent into exile until King Geumwa brought her to his palace in Buyeo. What happened next is well known: the king had her live in a separate wing of the palace,

6 〈신과 함께〉

where the sunlight followed her constantly until she became pregnant and gave birth to a large egg.

Exiled for falling in love with Haemosu, Yuhwa, the eldest daughter of the River God, had to survive by stealing fish from fishermen's nets. The reason she followed King Geumwa to Buyeo was probably because it was almost impossible for a woman to survive alone in those days. The sunlight that followed Lady Yuhwa in her secluded palace was a metaphor for Haemosu, with whom she secretly reunited. She became pregnant and gave birth to an egg from which a child hatched. Once again, Haemosu abandoned her without taking any responsibility. One can imagine how stressful it must have been for Lady Yuhwa to remain in the palace even after giving birth to another man's child.

> The mother decided to raise the child (母姑擧而養).
> After a month, he started talking (經月言語始).
> He said that a fly sucking on his eye (自言蠅嚐目)
> prevented him from sleeping well at night (臥不能安睡).
> His mother made him a bow and arrow (母爲作弓矢).
> He never missed his target (其弓不虛掎).

From the moment he was born, Lady Yuhwa's child was different. The boy was hatched from an egg and began to speak less than a month after his birth. He claimed that he could not sleep because of a fly, so his mother made him a bow and arrow. The importance of the bow and arrow to the ancient kings of the notheastern Asian region is evident from the fact that in Buyeo, "Jumong" was a word meaning "skilled archer," and she took it as her son's name. Therefore, archery was one of the basic skills expected of a hero. Lady Yuhwa had recognized her son's potential and made him a bow and arrow so that he could develop his archery and war skills from an early age.

Jumong grew up with the seven sons of King Geumwa. Unfortunately, none of them could become as exceptional as Jumong, no matter how hard they tried. Feeling that Jumong was a threat to them, they tormented him in all sorts of ways, constantly urging their father to get rid of him. However, King Geumwa was a broad-minded man with a heroic disposition who knew better than to believe everything his foolish sons told him. He had Jumong take care of the horses in the stables and waited to see if Jumong was really capable of rebelling against Buyeo as they claimed. Jumong could not help but feel humiliated by the task of caring for the horses, as his mother had taught him from an early age to be proud of his birth. He confessed to his mother, "I am a descendant of heaven, and yet I am tending horses for others. Life seems no better than death. I want to go south to build a kingdom of my own, but I can't leave you alone for my own sake.

Upon hearing these words, his mother (其母聞此言)
Wiping away her flowing tears, she said (潸然抆淸淚)

Don't mind me (汝幸勿爲念)
It always breaks my heart to see you suffer (我亦常痛痞).
She said a man going on a long journey (士之涉長途)
Needs a fine horse (須必憑騄駬)
And she took her son to the stable (相將往馬閑).
When she brandished a long whip (卽以長鞭捶)
All the horses ran away (群馬皆突走)
Except for one red horse (一馬騂色斐)
It jumped over a 12-foot fence (跳過二丈欄).
And she could tell that it was a fine horse (始覺是駿驥).

Lady Yuhwa said to her son, "A man of great strength needs the finest horse for a long journey, and I can find one for you." She went to the stable and brandished a long whip and all the horses ran away except one red horse that jumped over a 12-foot fence. When she found the most valuable horse, she stuck a needle under its tongue. The horse became thin because it could not swallow any food.

When King Geumwa came to look around the stable, he was pleased to see that many of the horses had become plump and gave the thin horse to Jumong as a reward. After the king left, Jumong removed the needle from under the horse's tongue and began to take good care of it. While other sources, including the *History of the Three Kingdoms*, mention Jumong as the one who chose the horse, the *Saga of King Dongmyeong* reveals that it was Lady Yuhwa who chose the horse for her son.

Lady Yuhwa was very determined when she ordered her son to leave, to make sure that he would not hesitate because of her. So, Jumong set out with like-minded friends, including Oi, Mari, and Hyeopbo. When they reached a river called Eomchaesu (淹滯水), with the Buyeo troops on their heels, they panicked to find that there were no boats in sight to cross the river to escape. This is where Jumong's family origin came in handy. Habaek may have banished his daughter for dating a man not arranged for her, but when he saw his grandson in danger, he sent fish and turtles to form a bridge so that Jumong could cross the river to safety. This scene is considered by scholars to be a dramatic depiction of the actual escape, in which Jumong and his friends crossed the river in winter when it was frozen, and the Buyeo troops failed to catch them because the river had already thawed by the time they reached it.

Jumong was fleeing in such a hurry that he left behind a pouch of barley seeds that his mother had given him. Lady Yuhwa had prepared five pouches for her son's long journey, each containing different seeds, but he had forgotten the one with the barley seeds. It was only after he had fought off the Buyeo troops that he realized this as he sat under a large tree to rest.

> A pair of pigeons carrying barley (雙鳩含麥飛)
> Came flying as messengers of Divine Mother (來作神母使).

When Jumong saw a pair of pigeons flying toward him, he believed that his divine mother must have sent them with the barley seeds. He shot an arrow, which knocked the two pigeons down and removed the barley seeds from their throats. He then splashed water on the pigeons, reviving them so that they could fly away.

In this way, *Saga of King Dongmyeong* portrays Lady Yuhwa as more than an ordinary daughter, wife, or mother. The fact that she made a bow and arrow for her son and chose a fine horse for him suggests that she had military acumen, quick judgment, and strong drive, all qualities of a good leader. As the daughter of the River God, she was well aware of the importance of water for agriculture, and she had the foresight to prepare grain seeds for her son so that his kingdom could prosper by expanding agriculture.

These rare and noble qualities of Lady Yuhwa were widely recognized by the Goguryeo people of that time. In the *Record of the Three Kingdoms*,[7] which describes the circumstances of the mid-third century, the part entitled "*Book of Wei: Biographies of Eastern Barbarians*"[8] has a section about Goguryeo. According to this section, there was a large cave called Gukdongdaehyeol[9] located east of Goguryeo's capital, where the god of water was worshipped. Such a cave actually exists east of Gungnae Fortress, the second capital of

---

7 『三國志』

8 『魏書』「東夷傳」

9 國東大穴

Goguryeo. It is large enough to hold a number of people, and there is a rock inside that seems to have served as an altar. From the entrance, one can see North Korea, just across the Aprok River.

The large cave to the east of the state, the Aprok River flowing in front of the cave, and Gungnae Fortress downstream are reminiscent of a scene based on details described in historical sources. The Goguryeo people used to hold a harvest ceremony called Dongmaeng.[10] Everyone would participate in an ancestral memorial ritual to the heavens, and then escort the water god brought out of the cave to a boat bound for Gungnae Fortress for a worship service in the capital. The ceremony was probably intended to unite the people of Goguryeo through the worship of their ancestors and his mother.

It is said that when the Tang emperor Taizong attacked and seized Yodong Fortress, there was a shrine to the guardians of Goguryeo, where Jumong and his mother were also worshipped. As the founding myth of Goguryeo spread both within and outside the state, Lady Yuhwa became deified as the divine mother of Goguryeo, and this continued until the fall of the kingdom. From the fourth century, the Goguryeo king called himself "Son of Heaven and Descendant of Habaek"[11] to emphasize the sacredness of his status. Just as the people idolized Lady Yuhwa rather than Jumong's father Haemosu, the kings also chose to be associated with her and her father Habaek.

10 東盟

11 天帝之子河伯之孫

Even after Jumong fled and founded Goguryeo on the Aprok River, Lady Yuhwa chose to stay in eastern Buyeo. She died in 24 BCE, the 14th year of King Dongmyeong's reign. King Geumwa held a funeral worthy of a queen mother and built a shrine to honor Lady Yuhwa's memory. Even though Jumong had once been a source of political strife in Buyeo and had eventually betrayed him, King Geumwa sent Lady Yuhwa off with a grand funeral, which speaks to the king's noble character and benevolence. Lady Yuhwa was also a loyal woman worthy of respect, as she remained by his side until the day she died.

Lady Ye, the Hero Maker from Buyeo

While Lady Yuhwa was undoubtedly the woman who influenced Jumong the most, his wives Lady Ye and Soseono also had a significant impact on him. Lady Ye married Jumong while he was still in Buyeo. She has only a brief appearance in the myth, setting up a chance for her son, Yuri on his journey to Goguryeo to be with his father when he founds out who his real father was. Because she is mentioned so briefly in the story, there is no way of knowing who Lady Ye really was or what her role was. The fact that her parents or family are never mentioned suggests that she was not from a prominent family.

Although she was pregnant at the time, Lady Ye did not stop her husband for her own sake when he made plans to flee Buyeo and establish a kingdom of his own. With her husband gone, she also had to endure political pressure from the other Buyeo princes, but still managed to raise her son Yuri to be a brave and capable man.

Yuri was a mischievous child. He would poke a hole in a water jar that a neighbor's wife wore on her head. He may have seemed to be idling away each day at an archery range, but in reality, he was acquiring the knowledge and skills expected of a ruler. His mother must have taught him self-discipline, otherwise he could not have made it to Goguryeo and succeeded his father on the throne. This suggests that Lady Ye must have been a wise, determined woman with a high level of self-esteem.

Soseono, the Heroine Behind the Foundations of Goguryeo and Baekje

After leaving his pregnant wife Lady Ye, Jumong went south to the middle region of the Aprok River and married a local woman named Soseono. Their marriage suggests that Goguryeo was formed by the union of two different groups, one led by Jumong from Buyeo and the other, a political force in the area in the middle region of the Aprok River.

Soseono appears in *History of the Three Kingdoms*, but in the section entitled "*Annals of Baekje*" rather than "*Annals of Goguryeo*." In addition, the section on King Onjo in *Annals of Baekje* offers two different stories about the marriage of Jumong and Soseono.

One is that Soseono was the second of three daughters of the king of Jolbon Buyeo (卒本扶餘), who had no sons. When the king met Jumong, he realized that he was no ordinary man and made him his second son-in-law. Shortly after the marriage, the king died and Jumong succeeded him. Jumong then used his position as ruler of Jolbon Buyeo to become the leader of a confederation of local tribes called Goguryeo. Jumong and Soseono had two sons, Biryu (沸流) and Onjo (溫祚).

According to the second story, Soseono was the daughter of a Jolbon man named Yeon Ta-bal (延陀勃). She married Wutae (優台), whose father was the son of a concubine of King Hae Bu-ru in northern Buyeo, and the couple had two sons named Biryu and Onjo. When Jumong fled from Buyeo, she contributed generously to the establishment of Goguryeo, so Jumong favored her and treated her sons Biryu and Onjo as his own. It is unclear from these two stories whether Jumong was the biological father of Biryu and Onjo. What is clear, however, is that Soseono played an important role in Jumong's establishment of Goguryeo.

Later, when Yuryu (孺留) or Yuri, Jumong's son with Lady Ye, came to his father from Buyeo, Jumong made him crown prince, and the throne passed to him after Jumong's death. At that time, Biryu told his younger brother Onjo, "When the king first escaped the oppression of Buyeo and came here, our mother used her family wealth to support him in establishing this great kingdom. But despite her tremendous support and service, he gave the kingdom to Yuryu. Instead of feeling useless and frustrated here, wouldn't it be better for us to take our mother and find a place in the south to build our own capital?"

Onjo agreed, and the brothers led a group of people to settle on the banks of the Han River. Soseono went with them and helped them build Baekje. She was 30 years old when she supported Jumong in founding Goguryeo, 49 when she supported her sons in founding Baekje, and 61 when she died in 6 BCE, the 13th year of King Onjo's reign. The age of forty-nine was considered very old in those days, but Soseono did not hesitate to go with her sons when they decided to leave Goguryeo and risk it all to establish a new kingdom.

These actions of hers made Soseono different from Lady Yuhwa or Lady Ye. Recognizing Jumong's potential, even though he had come from Buyeo with nothing and no one to rely on, she devoted all of her wealth and skills to making him king. Despite her powerful position as queen, she gave up her privileges and willingly participated in the arduous process of establishing another kingdom in the south. Considering this, we can say that Soseono achieved as much as Jumong or Onjo. However, her achievements have not been properly recognized in history and her activities have not been described in detail.

Soseono played a leading role in the establishment of Goguryeo and Baekje because of her clear judgment and great determination. Perhaps more light will be shed on her achievements in the future when the activites of women can be recognized as those of an individual human being rather than a woman.

2.
A Kingmaker: Queen Wu

Some people joke that history is "his story," i.e., a story in which the main characters are mostly men. Women are rarely the protagonists, and even when they are, the stories are still mostly about men. When Confucian ideas are added to the mix, the role of female protagonists is reduced or distorted to varying degrees. This is essentially what happened to the story of Lady Yuhwa mentioned above. Prior to the 17th century, before Confucian ideas had taken root in Korean society, the role, status, mentality, and behavior of women, as well as the general perceptions of women in society, were quite different from what we commonly think. This was also the case with Queen Wu, the wife of King Gogukcheon[12] and King Sansang.[13]

12 故國川王

13 山上王

The Rebellion of the Four Yeon Subtribes

Lady Wu became queen in the second month of 180, the second year of King Gogukcheon's reign. The *History of the Three Kingdoms* states that she was the daughter of Wu So (于素) of the Je tribe, or Je "nabu."[14] However, the name "Je nabu" seems to be a mistake made when the letters were engraved on the block, as the tribe was actually called "Yeon nabu."[15]

In the ninth month of 190, the 12th year of King Gogukcheon's reign, the king learned that two of the queen's relatives Eobiryu (於畀留) and Jwagaryeo (左可慮), who served as Jungwoedaebu (中畏大夫) of rank paeja (沛者) and as pyeongja (評者) respectively, were in the habit of abusing their privileges. Hearing this, the king became angry and decided to have them killed, and Jwagaryeo attempted an uprising with four Yeon sub-tribes. Through this record, we can understand that "Je nabu" is an incorrect spelling of "Yeon nabu".

After suppressing this attempted rebellion by the queen's relatives, King Gogukcheon decided to appoint people to run state affairs on the basis of talent rather than family background. On the recommendation of Anryu, he appointed Eulpaso (乙巴素), a farmer from Jwamulchon near the Aprok River, to Guksang,[16] which is equivalent

14 提那部

15 椽那部

16 國相

to today's Prime Minister. This system of meritocracy helped Goguryeo to take a step forward.

However, there was one person who was troubled by this change, and that person was none other than Queen Wu. The fact that she was not deposed despite her relatives' attempts at revolt shows just how powerful the Yeon nabu was at this time. But how did the Yeon nabu become so powerful in the first place?

The Tribe of Queens and Prime Ministers

Five political groups called "nabu" (那部) were at the center of Goguryeo's founding: Gyerubu (桂婁部), Biryu nabu (沸流那部), Yeon nabu (椽那部), Gwan nabu (灌奴部), and Hwan nabu (桓那部). These nabus are mentioned in Chinese historical sources such as *Record of Three Kingdoms* and *Book of the Hu Han*[17] as Gyerubu, Sonobu, Jeollobu, Gwannobu, and Sunnobu. Previously, these nabus were small independent states that had formed a local confederation to respond collectively to wars or to trade with outside powers.

Before Jumong came down from Buyeo, there was already a political group called Goguryeo in the central Aprok River area. This was the Goguryeo-hyeon of Hyeondogun (玄菟郡, Xuantu Commandery),

17 『後漢書』

which had been established in 107 BCE. In other words, there was already a Goguryeo before the one founded by Jumong. However, this Goguryeo was not a single small state that developed into a kingdom like Silla, but a local federation of several small states.

The leading independent state in this federation formed before Jumong's arrival was Biryuguk,[18] ruled by King Songyang.[19] Jumong arrived, competed with Songyang, and eventually replaced him as the leader of Biryuguk. This led to the formation of the second Goguryeo confederation, which is described in the *History of the Three Kingdoms* as the founding of Goguryeo in 37 BCE.

Although the Goguryeo kings of Gyerubu, who preceded Jumong and King Yuri, governed the federation along with the founding powers, they also sought to create policies that would strengthen their own power as kings. The powers that joined the federation lost their independence once they became subjects of the king, but they still strove to defend their vested rights. Internally, Goguryeo developed through a process of constant push and pull between the king, who intended to strengthen his authority, and the nobles, who sought to preserve their vested rights. This process eventually culminated with a concentration of power in the king.

Before the centralization of power in Goguryeo, the five nabus ran their own internal affairs semi-independently while cooperating

---

18 沸流國

19 松讓王

in external affairs. This nabu-based system was maintained from the reign of King Daemusin until the late third century, and it was during this period that King Gogukcheon ascended the throne. Therefore, it was highly unusual for the king to create a position Guksang and appoint a man like Eulpaso to fill it. The king would have faced serious opposition from the nobles had it not been for the attempted revolt by the four Yeon subtribes, which gave him an excuse to move forward with the reform.

Nevertheless, the Yeon nabu still enjoyed great power strategically granted by the king. Although Jumong, a mere immigrant from Buyeo, had succeeded in replacing King Songyang of Biryuguk as the leader of the Goguryeo Federation, the local political base of this royal family from Gyerubu could not match that of Songyang. For this reason, King Yuri made great efforts to strengthen and expand his political base by constantly going on hunting trips, taking several wives, and moving the capital. During King Daemusin's reign, the king himself led an attack on Buyeo and killed its ruler, thereby strengthening his own authority as king. Thus, King Daemusin was able to reorganize all the semi-independent powers under his control into a nabu-based system, which evolved into the system of five nabus during the reign of King Taejo.

Biryu nabu (the former Biryuguk, called Sonnobu in the *Record of Three Kingdoms*), as the original leading power within the confederation, remained threatening the kings until the middle of the third century.

It maintained its own ancestral shrine and held rites to worship the deities of agriculture and the land. To weaken Biryu nabu's power, the king and the royal family intermarried with people from Yeon nabu, or Jeollobu, for generations to strengthen the power of both Yeon nabu and the king. This strategy worked to a certain extent, but it eventually had some negative side effects.

In 165, Myeongnim Dapbu (明臨答夫) of Yeon nabu staged a coup by assassinating King Chadae (次大王) and enthroning King Sindae in his place, taking the position of Guksang. From then on, all queens and Guksangs came from Yeon nabu, and the tribe became overly powerful.

Though she was not deposed, Queen Wu must have felt uncomfortable with the failed revolt of the four Yeon subtribes. But then something happened that allowed her to turn things around. After ruling Goguryeo for 19 years, King Gogukcheon died without leaving a will or a crown prince, let alone any descendants. Queen Wu did not fail to take advantage of this opportunity.

The Queen of Two Kings

On the night that King Gogukcheon died, Queen Wu snuck out of the palace alone and went to King Gogukcheon's younger brother Balgi's house. When Balgi could not understand why his sister-in-law was visiting him late at night, Queen Wu said, "Since the king has no descendants, you should succeed him if anything happens to him." Displeased, Balgi snapped at her, "Fate is not to be discussed lightly, for it is determined by heaven and has its own course. Besides, how can that be an acceptable reason for a lady like you to wander about at night?"

Queen Wu was ashamed, but soon pulled herself together and went to her second brother-in-law Yeonu's house. Yeonu was equally surprised by her visit, but assuming she had a reason for coming, he dressed appropriately, went to the front gate to greet her warmly, and showed her to a room where he ordered something to be prepared for her to eat and drink. After being humiliated by the obstinate Balgi, Queen Wu was relieved by Yeonu's hospitality and revealed the truth to him: "The king has passed away without leaving a son, and his eldest brother Balgi should be the one to succeed him. But Balgi was rude to me, as if I were plotting treason against the king. So, I came to see you instead."

Yeonu became even more polite. Thinking that she must be too upset to eat properly, he tried to cut the meat for her himself, but ended up cutting his own finger instead. The queen immediately untied the straps of her skirt and bound his finger. When she was ready to leave, she said to him, "It's so late, I'm afraid something unexpected might happen. Would you please escort me back to the palace?" Realizing what she meant, Yeonu immediately took her hand to walk back to the palace.

Early the next morning, Queen Wu lied and said that King Gogukcheon had left a will before he died, expressing his wish to leave the throne to Yeonu. The court officials had no choice but to crown Yeonu king, as they had no way of verifying whether she was telling the truth or not.

Upon hearing this news, Balgi became furious. He had his troops surround the palace and shouted at Yeonu, "When the elder brother dies, the eldest of the remaining brothers should naturally succeed him. You have done me a grave injustice by robbing me of my chance to ascend the throne. Come out immediately!" Yeonu, however, locked himself up in the palace and did not come out for three days. Moreover, the people refused to side with Balgi. With the odds stacked against him, Balgi fled with his wife and children to Liaodong. There he met the Eastern Han governor, Gongsun Du (公孫度), and asked if he could borrow troops from the governor. The Eastern Han commanderies had been under constant attack from Goguryeo, and now that their princes were engaged in conflict, Gongsun Du was happy to have the opportunity to take advantage of Goguryeo's internal strife and agreed to grant Balgi's request.

But when Balgi returned to attack Goguryeo with the Eastern Han forces, Yeonu sent his younger brother Gyesu to deal with them. Gyesu had fought and won against the Eastern Han troops before, and he easily defeated them again this time. He then pursued Balgi and the fleeing Eastern Han troops with his men. Seeing that Gyesu was following him, Balgi said to him, "Are you really willing to harm your own brother?" Gyesu replied, "It was a grave wrong for Yeonu to take the throne from you, but you are committing an even greater wrong by leading the enemy's troops to destroy your own country, all because you are blinded by rage. How will you face our ancestors when you die?" Filled with shame and remorse upon hearing his brother's painfully truthful words, Balgi ran away to Baecheon (裴川), where he slit his own throat and died. Gyesu wept aloud when he saw his brother's body, covered it with grass, and buried it before returning to the palace.

Yeonu was sad yet happy to hear the news and treated Gyesu to a drink. As they drank, he tried to figure out why Gyesu had cried when Balgi committed suicide, wondering if it meant Gyesu blamed him for his betrayal. Willing to risk death for speaking his mind, Gyesu told him, "Although the queen has chosen you to succeed to the throne according to the late king's will, you should refuse out of decency. The fact that you didn't means that you never really had any love or respect for your brothers. I retrieved Balgi's body and buried it to demonstrate your virtues. I did not know that this was going to upset you. If you can wisely forget Balgi's misdeeds and give him a proper burial, how could anyone dare to question your righteousness? And now that I've told you what's on my mind, I don't care whether I live or die, so I ask you to execute me in front of the court officials." The look on Yeonu's face softened and he replied, "I was foolish enough to doubt you. Listening to what you said, I've realized the mistakes I made. I hope you don't blame yourself." Then they bowed to each other and had a round of drinks together. In the ninth month of that year, Yeonu, or King Sansang, gave the order to have Balgi's body unearthed and to hold a proper funeral for him in Baeryeong (裴嶺). Afterwards, he made Lady Wu his queen, as she was the one who helped him take the throne.

Queen Mother of King Dongcheon

The night her first husband, King Gogukcheon, died, Queen Wu risked her fate on Yeonu and became queen again. She still had no children, but in 228 she became the queen mother of King Dongcheon. King Dongcheon was Gyoche (郊彘), the son of King Sansang's concubine,[20] who was a peasant woman from the village of Jutongchon (酒桶村). But why did King Dongcheon name Queen Wu as his queen mother instead of his own biological mother?

When the Jutongchon woman was pregnant with King Sansang's child, Queen Wu sent an assassin to kill her and her baby. However, the woman was clever enough to save herself and her unborn child.

---

20 少后

When King Sansang learned of the assassination attempt, he pleaded with Queen Wu and convinced her not to harm them again. However, Queen Wu could not shake the fear that Gyoche would eliminate her once he ascended the throne. After much deliberation, she decided to test the crown prince's character. If he showed even a hint of malice, she would have to get rid of him, no matter what the cost.

The queen waited for the crown prince to leave the palace to play. One day in his absence, she had someone shave the mane off his horse. Most people would be furious to find their horse in such a state, but when the Crown Prince returned and saw it, he simply commented, "My horse looks so sad without its mane." On another occasion, Queen Wu had a servant spill soup on the Crown Prince's clothes while serving him his meal. Such an offense could have been punished with a whipping, but instead of losing his temper, the Crown Prince calmed the servant by telling him that he was fine.

These reactions assured Queen Wu that Gyoche had a kind and gentle personality. Thus, convinced that he would not harm her, she did not try to stand in his way when he ascended the throne. In fact, she may have even helped him, which could explain why he made her Queen Mother. Not only did Lady Wu become queen twice, but she was also personally involved in having two kings enthroned.

Lady Wu's Death and Changes in Goguryeo Society

Although she had enjoyed great power for a long time, there was still one thing that troubled Queen Wu. On her deathbed in the ninth month of 234, she said, "I have committed an immoral act, so how will I face Gugyang (國壤)? If the court officials hesitate to push me into the abyss, please bury me next to King Sansang's tomb." Gugyang was the name of King Gogukcheon.

In Goguryeo, married couples were buried in the same tomb. In large mound tombs, such as Taewangneung and the Tomb of the General, two platforms were placed side by side in the main chambers so that coffins could be placed on both. If someone died before his or her spouse, he or she was buried in the stone chamber, and the chamber doors were kept closed until the remaining spouse died. Some tombs have been found with three coffin platforms, probably for men with two wives or women with two husbands. It is interesting to note that one platform is usually larger than the other two, which are identical in shape and size. One of the murals inside Muyongchong depicts an everyday scene involving the tomb's owner, a man with two women sitting next to him side by side. The two women are the man's wives, and the fact that there is no difference in their position or size in the painting suggests that there was no discrimination between the two women. In other words, while there may have been first and second wives in Goguryeo, in terms of the time of marriage, there was no idea of distinguishing between the legal wife and concubines as there would be later in Joseon.

To return to the story of Queen Wu, King Dongcheon granted Queen Wu her last wish regarding her burial. The problem was that this violated Goguryeo burial customs. Levirate marriage (i.e., the marriage of a deceased man's widow to his surviving brother) was practiced in Goguryeo, but although a widow could marry her deceased husband's brother, she was supposed to be buried next to her first husband after her death. Queen Wu, however, wished to be buried next to her second husband, King Sansang, and King Dongcheon granted it.

Then a strange thing happened. The day after the Queen Mother's funeral, a shaman came to King Dongcheon to deliver the words of King Gogukcheon: "Yesterday I was so angry that I couldn't bear to see Lady Wu go to sleep with King Sansang. I went over and argued with her. Now that I am back in my tomb and thinking about it, I feel so ashamed that I cannot face the people, so discuss this matter with the court officials and set up an obstacle to block my view." In accordance with his words, seven rows of pine trees were planted in front of Gogukcheon's tomb. In this way, Queen Wu was able to do things that no one else could do, both in life and in death.

This incident indicates a major change that had taken place in Goguryeo society. Let's reflect on the words that Queen Wu spoke on her deathbed. She said, "I have committed an immoral act, so how will I face Gukyang?" By "immoral act," she may not have meant the lie she had told about King Gogukcheon's will that helped Yeonu succeed to the throne as King Sansang. Rather, she may have been referring to the fact that she had married her brother-in-law after her husband's death. If so, her words suggest that by this time, levirate marriage was no longer common in Goguryeo society and had become an outlawed practice.

Levirate marriage was a distinctive custom of northern Asian tribes such as the Xiongnu (匈奴). If a man died on the battlefield, his wife and children were unlikely to survive on their own, so the man's brother was expected to take them in. This, however, was considered highly immoral from the perspective of Confucian beliefs. Scholars interpret Queen Wu's comment as a sign that Goguryeo had changed from a nomadic, hunting society to an agricultural one, and that Confucian ethics had been introduced. In any case, Queen Wu seems to have had a dramatic life and death that left much to be discussed.

3. A Woman from Jutongchon: King Sansang's Beloved

The Desire for a Son Leads to Jutongchon

As the second younger brother of King Gogukcheon, King Sansang had never been first in line to the throne. Queen Wu was the only reason he was able to be crowned king, and so he made her his queen instead of taking another wife upon his enthronement. The couple failed to conceive, however, and the king's desire for a son to succeed him grew stronger with each passing year. In the third month of 203, he prayed to the mountains and streams of nature. The heavens must have heard his desperate plea, because on the night of the 15th of that month he had a dream telling him not to worry, because his concubine would bear him a son.

The problem was that he had no concubine at that time. When

he awoke, King Sansang told his court officials about the dream and asked for their advice: "Heaven told me not to worry, but I have no concubine. What do you think I should do?" The officials did not know what to say, so Guksang Paso (巴素) replied on their behalf, "If this is the will of Heaven, you should have complete faith in it. All you have to do is wait with faith."

It took five years for the will of Heaven to be realized. In the eleventh month of 208, a pig that was to be sacrificed to heaven escaped and ran away. Alarmed, the man in charge of preparing the sacrificial items for the ritual chased after the pig, but catching it proved to be quite difficult. After running here and there, the pig disappeared in a village called Jutongchon. When the man chased it into the village, a beautiful girl who looked to be about 20 years old had caught the pig and handed it to him with a smile. The man thought it was strange that a young maiden had been able to get hold of the pig he had tried so hard to catch, and when he returned to the palace, he reported the incident to the king.

Since the pig was an offering to heaven, the king listened carefully to what the man said. He also found it strange, so he changed into plain clothes and went to Jutongchon that night. When he arrived at the maiden's house, the king asked for her. When the maiden and her family realized that the unexpected visitor was the king, they could not turn him away. The maiden invited him into her room, where, in spite of the presence of the almighty king, she asked him in a low but firm voice to make her a promise: "I would not dream of defying you, but I would like you to promise me one thing. If I give birth to a boy, please do not abandon us. Promise that you will take us with you to the palace." The king agreed and took her in his arms. Then, around midnight, he got up and returned to his palace.

Gyoche is Born

In the third month of 209, Queen Wu learned that the king had been with a woman in Jutongchon. She was furious with jealousy. She secretly sent troops to kill the woman. The woman, however, got wind of the news and escaped by disguising herself as a man. Knowing only too well the punishment that awaited them if they failed to carry out the queen's orders, the troops searched desperately and finally captured the woman. But just as they were about to kill her, she suddenly said to them in a firm voice, "Is it the king or the queen who has ordered you to kill me? I am carrying the child of the king of Goguryeo. Do you really think that no harm will come to you if you kill the king's child?" After hearing these words, the troops were no longer able to carry out their mission. They feared the queen, but they feared the king even more. The troops returned to the palace and told the queen exactly what the woman had said. Queen Wu was even more enraged to learn that such a humble woman was carrying the child she and the king had so desperately wanted, and she was determined to kill her. However, she did not succeed.

When King Sansang heard this, he went to Jutongchon to meet the woman and said, “I have heard that you are expecting a child. Who is the father?” The woman replied, “I have never been alone in the same room even with my brothers, so how could I be intimate with a man? The child I am carrying is yours.” Thrilled by this reassurance, the king comforted the woman and generously rewarded her family with gifts. Upon returning to the palace, the king stressed to Queen Wu the necessity of having an heir to ensure the continuity of the royal family. He swore that he would never betray her under any circumstances and asked her to let the woman in Jutongchon give birth. A child was the one thing Queen Wu could not bring to the king, and she had no choice but to do as he asked.

In the ninth month of 209, the woman in Jutongchon gave birth to a baby boy. Overjoyed, King Sansang declared, “This child has been given to me by heaven as my son and heir.” King Sansang named his son Gyoche (meaning pig) because it was a pig offered to heaven that led him to meet the woman and have a child with her. He made the woman, Gyoche’s mother, as a concubine and had her live in the palace with her son, as he had promised. In the first month of 213, he proclaimed Gyoche crown prince. When he died in 227, Gyoche succeeded him and became King Dongcheon.

The Wise Woman from Jutongchon

The name of the woman from Jutongchon was Hunyeo (后女). When her mother was pregnant with her, a shaman had told her mother that she would give birth to a queen. Her mother was delighted and named her daughter Hunyeo, which means "the girl who will be queen." This shows that Hunyeo's mother was quite an ambitious and daring woman. Perhaps she expected the prophecy to come true.

The *Annals of King Sansang* in *History of the Three Kingdoms* mentions a woman called "the peasant girl of Jutongchon," but does not give her name. The name Hunyeo appears in the section on the year when King Dongcheon ascended the throne. It also says, "The mother (of King Dongcheon) was a woman from Jutongchon who came to the palace and became the concubine of King Sansang, but nothing is known about her family." It goes on to say that the woman's mother named her daughter Hunyeo after a shaman told her that she would give birth to a queen.

These details leave little doubt that King Sansang's concubine came from a humble family. Judging from the name "Jutongchon," the family may have lived in a village that specialized in brewing. In this case, the village may have been a bugok,[21] where the lowest class of people worked together in a particular profession, unlike ordinary

21 部曲

villages of common people. It is remarkable that a woman who lived in such a village had the audacity to name her daughter Hunyeo! So she was no ordinary woman, and neither was her daughter, who convinced the troops to disobey the queen's order to kill her. From the way Hunyeo carried herself, it was almost as if her mother had taught her the manners and mentality of a queen to prepare her for the future.

On the night when King Sansang first visited Hunyeo and conceived a child with her, she showed a side of herself that was unlikely in someone of her humble background. Even later, in the face of the assassins sent by Queen Wu, she never lost her composure. The way she handled crises and said what was necessary in each situation shows that she was indeed a wise woman.

Was it really the will of Heaven that caused King Sansang to make a woman of such inferior birth his concubine? The Chinese history book, *Book of Wei*, says that because King Sansang was childless, he slept with a Gwanno (灌奴) woman who bore him a son. Gwanno refers to the Gwan nabu that is mentioned in the *History of the Three Kingdoms*. In other words, Hunyeo was a woman from Jutongchon who belonged to Gwan nabu.

Gwan nabu was one of the five nabus, or tribes, behind the founding of Goguryeo. However, it was less prominent than Gyerubu, from which the royal family originated, or Biryu nabu, the original leading power within the Goguryeo Federation, or Yeon nabu, which produced queens and prime ministers. Miyu (彌儒), who held the rank of paeja from Gwan nabu, was recognized for his contribution to the enthronement of King Chadae.[22] Eojiryu (菸支留) of Hwan nabu, who served as the rank of wutae (于台), and Yangsin (陽神) of Biryu nabu, who served as the rank of joui (皂衣), were also close to King Chadae. These three men were appointed as either jwabo (左輔) or jungwoedaebu after King Chadae ascended the throne. Jwabo was the highest position at the time, so when it was given to Miyu, it meant an advance in status for Gwan nabu, albeit one that only lasted until the coup orchestrated by Myeongnim Dapbu (明臨答夫) removed King Chadae from the throne and replaced him with King Sindae.

Queen Wu of Yeon nabu, who had made him king, was so powerful that King Sansang was not really free to take another woman as his concubine, even though she could not produce an heir. Under these circumstances, the best way for the king to enhance his power was to empower one of the weaker nabus, gain its political support, and take a concubine from that nabu to bear him a son and a successor. This is probably why King Sansang was so eager and determined to meet a woman from a weaker nabu.

Queen Wu's greatest weakness was her inability to produce an heir. She had failed to conceive with both of her husbands, so she was in no position to object to a concubine who had given her second

22 次大王

husband a son. The prophecy that Hunyeo's mother received from a shaman was most likely a story created later to emphasize that Hunyeo had always been destined to be a queen.

In any case, Hunyeo lived up to her name by becoming a concubine and living to see her son, the crown prince, ascend to the throne. Despite growing up in a palace where he had to be constantly aware of the powerful Queen Wu, King Dongcheon proved to be a gentle and capable man. This was probably due to the education he received from his mother, Hunyeo. However, historical sources state that nothing is known about her family, meaning that her background was not judged to be worth mentioning, no matter how wise and graceful she was.

Instead of his biological mother, King Dongcheon made Lady Wu his queen mother. This proves not only how powerful Queen Wu and Yeon nabu were, but also how wise Hunyeo was. If Hunyeo had defied Queen Wu or plotted against her out of ambition or jealousy, she could have endangered her life and that of her son. She must have walked on eggshells in the palace because of Queen Wu, so one can imagine how difficult it must have been for her to keep her son safe there. This case contrasts with that of the concubine who will be introduced in the next chapter.

4.
A Long-haired Concubine Thrown Away to the Sea: Lady Gwanna

King Jungcheon and Queen Yeon

In the fourth month of 251, King Jungcheon[23] ordered Lady Gwanna (貫那夫人) to be put in a leather bag and thrown into the Yellow Sea. Lady Gwanna was a fair-skinned woman with hair nearly three meters long, and her long, silky hair rippled with every step she took. The king was so enamored of this woman that he brought her to live in the palace and planned to make her his concubine.

His queen at that time was Lady Yeon (椽氏). He had married her in the tenth month of 248. Yeon was not the queen's surname. It was taken from the first syllable of Yeon nabu, where she came from. The

23 中川王

royal family is said to have used Go (高) as a family name since the reign of Goguryeo's founder, Dongmyeong the Holy. The tradition of choosing the king's wife from Yeon nabu began during the reign of his grandfather, King Sansang, and continued until the time of King Jungcheon.

To return to the story of the queen, Queen Yeon feared that the long-haired beautiful Lady Gwanna was monopolizing the king's affections and wanted her out of the palace. So one day she said to the king, "I have heard that the Western Wei (西魏) are looking for a long-haired beauty and are willing to pay a fortune for her. In the past, one of our kings was invaded by China because he neglected to send gifts and almost lost his kingdom. If you send an envoy to offer them the long-haired beauty, they will gladly accept, and we will never be attacked again."

The invasion she was referring to was the fall of Hwando Fortress to a Wei army led by Guanqiu Jian (毌丘儉). King Dongcheon had fled to southern Okjeo and then on to northern Okjeo as the Wei army continued to chase him. He was forced to flee as far as Sushen and barely made it back alive. King Jungcheon realized that Queen Yeon's plot to send Lady Gwanna to China was driven by jealousy. He was furious that she would use his father's humiliating past to achieve her goal, but he bit his tongue.

Lady Gwanna's Unsuccessful Countermove

When Lady Gwanna heard what Queen Yeon had said to King Jungcheon, she began to panic, thinking that the queen might try to harm her. She had yet to give birth to a prince or become a concubine, which meant that the queen and her powerful family could try to get rid of her at any time.

So, Lady Gwanna decided to set the Queen up. She told the King a lie: "The Queen keeps asking what a country girl like me is doing here in the palace. She has cursed me and threatened to make me regret it if I do not leave of my own accord. I think she will harm me in your absence, so what should I do?" Again, King Jungcheon chose not to answer and instead went hunting in Gigu (箕丘).

When the king returned to the palace, Lady Gwanna greeted him with a leather sack in her hands. Sobbing, she told him, "The queen tried to put me in this sack and throw me into the sea. I beg you to let me go home. It's the only way I can stay alive. How can I continue to serve you in these circumstances?" Unfortunately for her, the king soon found out that this was a lie, and angrily told her, "I suppose you really want to jump into the sea." Then he ordered her to be put in a sack and thrown into the sea.

Why Did Lady Gwanna End up in the Sea?

The *Annals of King Jungcheon* in *History of the Three Kingdoms* only say that when Lady Gwanna falsely accused the queen of trying to put her in a leather sack and throw her into the sea, the king became enraged and ordered that she be thrown into the sea. However, the many details of what happened in between seem to be missing from the *History of the Three Kingdoms*.

When the king heard Lady Gwanna's accusation against the queen, he must have been furious at first. He probably went to the queen to rebuke her with a stern warning. The queen must have been humiliated to hear the false accusation against her. The Guksang and other court officials would then have convinced the king of the need to investigate such a serious accusation. The maids and servants of the queen and Lady Gwanna must have been summoned and interrogated, eventually leading to the conclusion that Lady Gwanna had attempted to manipulate the king.

This incident must have seriously damaged the king's authority and hampered his efforts to consolidate his power as a political leader. Earlier in his reign, King Jungcheon had uncovered and crushed a revolt led by his brother Yemul (預勿). The details of the plot and the reason for it remain unknown, but the king may have been forced to ask the powerful Guksang Myeongnim Eosu (明臨於漱) of Yeon nabu for help in suppressing the revolt. He seems to have repaid the favor in 250 by putting Myeongnim Eosu in charge of the kingdom's armed forces. This would have made the queen, the Guksang, and other Yeon nabu government officials even more powerful than before.

King Jungcheon may have remembered how his grandfather, King Sansang, had taken a concubine from Gwan nabu and fathered a son by her in order to maintain the balance of power with Queen Wu. So, when he came across this beautiful, long-haired girl from Gwan nabu, he brought her to his palace to make her his concubine. The beautiful woman was immediately intimidated by the queen's initial threats. She decided to make an accusation against her, which turned out to be a fabrication. At first, King Jungcheon believed what Lady Gwanna had told him. He turned the palace inside out to find out the truth. If he did nothing to restore his damaged reputation, his ability to conduct affairs of state would be undermined. The king had no choice but to put Lady Gwanna in a leather bag and throw her into the sea. To preserve his authority as king, he had to hold back his tears and sacrifice the woman he loved. These details are, of course, derived from what is only briefly mentioned in the historical sources.

Although both women were from Gwannabu and had to struggle to survive in the domestic political environment of Goguryeo, Hunyeo, the concubine of King Sansang and the birth mother of King Dongcheon, and the long-haired Lady Gwanna met very different ends. Hunyeo responded wisely to the challenges she faced and enjoyed the privilege of giving birth to a king. Lady Gwanna, on the other hand, reacted unwisely to the queen's threat and was eventually executed by the king.

5.
A Princess Who Chose a Fool: Pyeonggang

Princess Pyeonggang was the daughter of King Pyeongwon, the 25th king of Goguryeo. Koreans tend to remember her as the tearful princess who married Ondal the Fool. Princess Pyeonggang has been recorded in history only through Ondal, to the point that it is almost impossible to think of her without the foolish Ondal. In the *History of the Three Kingdoms*, it is also written not as the "*Story of Princess Pyeoggang*" but as the "*Story of Ondal*." This title seems to imply that the princess is not the main character, but plays a secondary role in the story as Ondal's wife.

Surprisingly, however, she remains a central character until halfway through the story. As a little girl, Princess Pyeonggang was such a crybaby that her father used to threaten to marry her off to Ondal the Fool. When she turned 16, her father arranged for her to marry a Mr.

Go of Sangbu (上部高氏). The princess refused because her father always said that Ondal would be her husband. Enraged, the king shouts, “If you won’t do as I say, then get out!” The princess left the palace and went straight to Ondal’s house. Ondal and his mother tried to turn her away because of their different backgrounds, but the princess convinced them persistently until they finally changed their minds. After the couple’s marriage, Princess Pyeonggang continued to have a central role in the story, selling her gold bracelets to buy the land, the house, the servant, the horse and the ox, among other things.

Ondal only begins to play an active role in the second half of the story. On the 3rd of the third month, he excelled in a hunting competition held on a hill in Nangnang Commandery. Furthermore, when the Northern Zhou invaded Liaodong, Ondal led the Goguryeo troops to victory. The king finally recognized him as his son-in-law and gave him the rank of Daehyeong (大兄). Ondal went on to fight against Silla during the reign of King Yeongyang and was killed in battle.

Princess Pyeonggang, however, left another mark on the story’s finale. Just before leaving for war with Silla, Ondal declared: “We will not return until we have reclaimed the lands of Gyerip-hyeon and the west of Jukryeong!” Sadly, Ondal was killed by an arrow flying out of nowhere during a battle below Adan Fortress. At his funeral, when his coffin was carried to his grave, it could not be moved. Princess Pyeonggang came over and caressed the coffin, saying, “Alas! We have no control over life and death, so come, it is your time to go." With these words, the coffin was lifted and the funeral continued. When the king heard this, he was heartbroken. This is where the story ends.

Considering the way the story unfolds and the importance of her role in it, it seems that the story should have been called "*The Story of Princess Pyeonggang*," not "*The Story of Ondal*." So why the discrepancy between the title and the story?

According to the story, Princess Pyeonggang was stubborn and very much her own woman. The fact that she cried so much that the king had to joke about marrying her to Ondal the Fool shows how headstrong she was from childhood. Then, at the age of 16, she defied her father's wishes and went all by herself to Ondal's house to propose marriage. When Ondal refused, she slept outside his house and went back the next day to persuade him and his mother. She had such a strong sense of self that she was willing to give up everything to marry the man of her choice. She also had the drive to persevere until she got what she wanted.

Princess Pyeonggang was a very practical woman, unlike fairy-tale princesses who spend their time adorning themselves in elegant palaces until a handsome suitor comes along to marry them. When she left the palace, she wore dozens of precious bracelets, which she sold to buy farmland, a house, a slave, a horse, an ox, and other goods. This suggests that she was quite familiar with how the economy and society worked outside the palace. She also seems to have had the ability to recognize good horses. When Ondal wanted to buy a horse, she advised him to buy one sold by the state rather than one sold by merchants in the market. This suggests that Princess Pyeonggang had military acumen, like Lady Yuhwa, the mother of the founder of Goguryeo.

She advised Ondal on his choice of horses and his training in archery, which led to his outstanding performance in the hunting competition and his great contributions on the battlefield. From this, we can see that Princess Pyeonggang seems to have played a major role in transforming Ondal into a General. It seems unlikely that a man who wandered around stripping the bark off elm trees to stave off hunger had any riding or archery skills before marrying the princess. Then how could a man like Ondal, who had been considered a fool by everyone for so long, including the king, become such an outstanding military commander? It would not have been possible without the well-organized education and training of Princess Pyeonggang. In other words, she was a person endowed with military acumen, good teaching skills, determination, and a strong sense of self.

Princess Pyeonggang was therefore not the sort of woman to remain in her husband's shadow. In fact, in Goguryeo society, women were not excluded from social activities, and there was no marked inequality between husbands and wives. Murals in Goguryeo tombs often depict couples going on outings or attending religious ceremonies together. In Goguryeo tombs, the coffin platforms for men and women tended to be the same size. At harvest ceremonies, men and women, young and old, enjoyed singing and dancing late into the night. The women of that time were not the same as those of the Joseon period, when there was a saying that if a hen crows, the family is ruined.

Why, then, did Princess Pyeonggang not use her superior family background and military skills to distinguish herself? Why did she instead choose to support her husband, Ondal, a simple fool? Could she have been a traditional woman who found meaning in supporting her husband and raising her children? Why did the princess portrayed in the history books stay out of the limelight and concentrate on improving her husband? The answer lies in the ideological foundation of the *History of the Three Kingdoms*, which tells the story of Princess Pyeonggang and Ondal. The *History of the Three Kingdoms* is a history book written from a Confucian point of view. According to the Confucian view of marriage, a husband is like heaven and his wife is like earth. A princess cannot be excluded from this view. In stories about married couples, the only way for the wife to come into the limelight is to be a good assistant to her husband. This version of the story of Princess Pyeonggang and Ondal has the same ideology.

It seems that a distortion in the process of creating a Confucian version of the story for *History of the Three Kingdoms* caused the inconsistency between the choices made by the princess in the first and second halves of the story. As the Confucian way of life completely changed Korean customs and mentality from the 17th century on-

Statue of Ondal and Princess Pyeonggang on Mt. Acha (above, © Kang Byeong Kee, Wikipedia) and Ondal Mountain Fortress in Danyang (below, © Chunga Publishing)

Some say that the Adan Fortress, where Ondal was killed, was located on present-day Mt. Acha, while others say that it was at the site of the Ondal Mountain Fortress in Danyang.

ward, Pyeonggang became a symbol of a woman to be admired, not a person in her own right.

However, from the time of the princess until the 16th century, women did not resemble the Confucian ideal of women in the Joseon dynasty. The women of the three ancient kingdoms and Goryeo were confident, proactive, and had a strong sense of self. This may be the true traditional image of Korean women, and this would make Princess Pyeonggang the most traditional of them. She may also be the most modern of the women. She had all the characteristics of a capable, self-confident working woman of modern times.

In some ways, however, she was not so modern. Most women today are competent and very much on their own, but many of them still dream of living like Cinderella rather than Princess Pyeonggang. Such women want to meet a prince charming in the hope that it will bring about an immediate rise in their own status. In a sharp contrast to that point of view, when Princess Pyeonggang proposed to Ondal, she said to him, “If we are really of the same mind, why wait until we become wealthy?” These words make her sound far from calculating and almost ignorant of the ways of the world, unlike today’s women in Korea. Today, more men want to be supported like Ondal, but there are few women willing to support them like Princess Pyeonggang. Perhaps this discrepancy is the reason why so many men and women have a hard time finding the right one these days.

6.
A Tang Captive's Sad Love Story: Okso

A Goguryeo Woman's Execution in Chang'an

The markets in the Tang capital of Chang'an were always bustling with people. In one market, exotic goods brought from the West along the Silk Road were stacked high, while in another market, food and groceries, including grains, fruits, fish, and meat from all over the country, lured people to the stalls. In yet another market, one might see fancy, seductive silk dresses and sheer shawls draped over bare shoulders, beckoning to women passing by. In addition to being the country's capital, Chang'an served as a hub for trade between East and West, and you could find just about anything in the city's markets. Naturally, all kinds of people flocked to the city, including Westerners, fur-hatted Turks, Khitans, Xianbeis, people from Silla, and even Japanese from across the sea.

Early one morning, workmen began erecting a wooden scaffold in the East Market of Chang'an. The scaffold had three wooden beams at the top, each with a noose hanging from it, indicating that three prisoners were about to be executed. Such an event was something that people in the market, either buyers or sellers, would not want to miss. Sure enough, before noon, the execution site was crowded with spectators.

At the sound of the gong at noon, the prisoners were finally dragged out by the guards. There were three of them, one woman and two men. It was easy to imagine how badly they had been tortured; their clothes were almost torn off, their hair was disheveled, and their faces and bodies were covered with dried blood. It was hard to tell what they normally looked like.

Dragged by the guards with her arms tied behind her back and limping, the woman, stumbled halfway, then staggered again as the guards roughly dragged her to her feet and barely made it up to the execution stake. The woman was a slave named Okso (玉素) and among the two men executed with her, one was a Goguryeo immigrant, and the other's background is unknown. Okso was accused of trying to poison her master, and the two unidentified men were accused of helping her escape.

A Captive Brought to Chang'an[24]

The story of Okso appears in Volume 5 of *Collected Records of the Court and Common People*[25] by Zhang Zuo (658–730) of Tang China. The story goes that there was a man named Guo Zhengyi (郭正一, ?–689) from Gucheng (鼓城) of Dingzhou, which is now Jinxian (晋縣) of Hebei-sheng. He received the title of jinshi (進士) during the reign of Emperor Taizong and served as Palace Secretary[26] and Imperial Scholar.[27] In 682, he was appointed the Chief Minister of the Council in the Central Administration.[28] From this time on, Tang chancellors were formally referred to as tong pingzhangshi. Zhengyi enjoyed power in high positions for years until he was framed during the reign of Empress Wu Zetian and exiled to the Lingnan region, where he was executed. The rest of his family lost everything they owned and got punished accordingly.

The beautiful slave who came into the possession of Guo Zhengyi as a result of the fall of Pyongyang Fortress was Okso. Historical sources do not mention whether Okso was originally a slave

24 The story of the Goguryeo immigrant Okso was introduced in a research paper I published in 2001 ["Situations of Goguryeo Emigrants," *The Journal of Korean Ancient History*, 23 (2001): 63–105]. This story has been adapted from the source *Chaoye qianzai* (『朝野僉載』).

25 『朝野僉載』

26 中書舍人

27 弘文館 學士

28 中書侍郎 同平章事

or whether she had previously been a commoner or a noblewoman. From the description that her beauty stood out even amid the chaotic fall of Pyongyang Castle, it seems most likely that she was a young lady from a noble family, with skin as fair as white marble wearing a silken gown. Zhengyi took Okso back to his home in Chang'an, where she gained enough trust from him to put her in charge of the storehouse where he kept his riches. This means that Okso was not only attractive, but also educated and clever, which makes it even more likely that she was a noblewoman. However, this task was not all that Zhengyi had in mind for Okso. He often enjoyed drinks and porridge at night, and whenever he had Okso bring him porridge, he took her to bed with him.

Stuck in such a living hell, Okso's face grew paler by the day. That was painful to watch, especially for a certain young man. He, too, was a Goguryeo immigrant who had met Okso on the street one day. He had fallen in love with her the moment he saw her. Okso also found comfort in him as she struggled to adjust to life in a foreign land. From time to time, the two would run into each other at a market while running errands and agree to meet somewhere nearby. The only person who knew about the young couple was a slave who tended to Zhengyi's horses. He may have been pleased at the sight of the lovely young couple.

As a slave, Okso was still unable to keep her master's hands off of her, and Zhengyi became more demanding by the day. This led to more and more abuse of Okso by Zhengyi's wife. Now that she had a lover, Okso could no longer stand it. One night, when Zhengyi asked for porridge again, Okso mixed some poison into the porridge and brought him the bowl. Zhengyi did not suspect anything at first, but it took only a few spoonfuls for him to notice that the porridge tasted strange. He shouted, "That slave bitch fed me poisoned porridge!" He then had a servant bring bean paste and licorice to detoxify him. When the commotion was over, everyone in the house began looking for Okso, but by then she was long gone. She had also taken about a dozen gold and silver items from the house with her.

Zhengyi reported the incident to the authorities. Upon hearing the news, the emperor personally ordered an experienced General in Chang'an named Bu Liang (不良) to conduct a thorough search for Okso. In the eyes of the emperor, the incident was not just a crime committed by a slave. It involved a Goguryeo immigrant and thus had the potential to encourage other immigrants to revolt. General Bu immediately searched the area for three days, but could not find the thief.

A commander named Wei Chang (魏昶) had an idea. He ordered his men to select three young decent slaves of Zhengyi, make them change into hemp clothes, and cover their heads with bamboo baskets. He then tied up four guards of Zhengyi and made them stand in front of the three slaves who were trembling with fear. He asked the guards if they had noticed anyone spying on Zhengyi's house recently. One of the guards confessed, "A Goguryeo immigrant gave me a letter, so I gave it to the slave who tended the horses. Here is the letter." The letter delivered by the guard contained only one sentence: "There is an empty house in Jincheng Ward." Bu Liang gave the order to search all the empty houses in Jincheng Ward. One of them turned out to have an elaborate padlock on the door, and when Bu Liang's men broke the lock and entered, they found Okso and a Goguryeo man hiding there. They were taken into custody, and after being brutally tortured, the Goguryeo man and Zhengyi's slave caring the horses confessed to helping Okso hide from the authorities. As a consequence, Okso and the two men were executed in the East Market.

Goguryeo Immigrants in Tang China

When Goguryeo fell, its people scattered in all directions. Fearing that they might try to revive Goguryeo, Tang forced about 190,000 of them to resettle in the interior of China. Some of the remaining people went to Silla, Japan, or the Turkic Empire. Those who remained in the former Goguryeo territories, such as the Liaodong region and the northwestern areas of the Korean peninsula, were mainly people without status or property. Wherever these former residents of Goguryeo went, the future was as unpredictable for them as it was for the people of a fallen kingdom.

The ruling class, however, fared somewhat better than others who went abroad. Nobles who had voluntarily surrendered, as well as the descendants of King Bojang, continued to enjoy privileges after surrendering to the Tang dynasty. Although they faced some discrimination, they were able to use their skills in the Tang Empire, where people were relatively open to different ethnicities. Some served the Tang emperor in close proximity, some helped demonstrate Tang's strength and glorify the emperor's virtues and dignity, and some helped support and govern the Goguryeo people who remained in the former territory of the fallen kingdom. The area in which the Goguryeo immigrants were most involved was military activities. The Tang court sought ways to effectively utilize outstanding military commanders of other ethnicities. For immigrants without power bases, the quickest way to climb the social ladder was to earn merit in the Tang army.

Even if they had surrendered to the Tang Empire, performed meritorious deeds in war, and risen to high positions, Goguryeo immigrants were not guaranteed a comfortable life and continuous advancement throughout their lives. They all faced challenges in establishing themselves and surviving in Tang society. Nobles had to be careful not to be betrayed by the people, and they had to fight endlessly on the battlefields to maintain their positions. As for commoners and slaves, they had to endure discrimination and oppression based on their social status and ethnicity, while also coping with poverty in an unfamiliar environment. Some struggled to make ends meet before resorting to crime and being executed. This is probably the reason why the average life span of Goguryeo immigrants was not very long.

As people who had lost their country, it was quite hard for anyone, let alone women, to survive in an enemy country. The same was clearly true for women like Okso, who became prisoners given as rewards to enemy Generals. No matter when or where it happens, war always inflicts great pain on women. It did so to Okso in the late seventh century, and it continues to do so to women in the twenty-first century. Fifteen hundred years have passed, but women's rights in war have not improved much.

Index

The diverse people who shaped an Ancient Kingdom

Men and Women of Goguryeo

Published on November 30, 2023
Written by Hyun-sook Kim
Publisher Young-ho Lee
Published by Northeast Asian History Foundation

Address 81, Tongil-ro, Seodaemun-gu, Seoul, Republic of Korea
Tel 02-2012-6065
Website www.nahf.or.kr
Printed in Nikebooks

ISBN 979-11-7161-015-0 03910